The Ultimate UK Low Cholesterol Cookbook for Beginners:

Over 2,500 Diet Recipe Variations for Heart Health. Enjoy Delicious, Nutritious Meals with a Simple, Affordable, and Stress-Free 31-Day Plan

Disclaimer
The information in this cookbook is intended for general guidance on low cholesterol diets and should not be considered as medical advice. The author is not a healthcare professional, and the content in this book is based on research and personal knowledge.

It is always recommended to consult a doctor or qualified healthcare provider before making any significant changes to your diet, especially if you have underlying health conditions or are on medication. The author and publisher disclaim any liability for adverse effects resulting from the use of the recipes or information in this book.

Table of Contents

Introduction

Welcome to my Low Cholesterol Diet Cookbook, where I've put together a range of simple, tasty, and nutritious recipes to help you enjoy a heart-healthy lifestyle without any fuss. I understand that eating well shouldn't be complicated or expensive, so I've made sure that each recipe is easy to follow and uses affordable ingredients you can find in your local shop.

These dishes are packed with flavour, and whether you're cooking for yourself or your family, you'll find plenty of options that are not only good for you but also a pleasure to eat. From quick breakfasts to satisfying dinners and even tempting desserts, I've made sure there's something for everyone.

I believe healthy eating should be enjoyable, so I hope this cookbook helps you discover how easy it can be to prepare meals that are both nourishing and delicious. Let's make low cholesterol living simple and satisfying!

Chapter 1: Understanding Cholesterol

Cholesterol is a fatty substance that your body needs in small amounts to function properly. However, having too much cholesterol can increase the risk of heart disease. One way to manage this is by being mindful of how much cholesterol you consume each day.

Health guidelines suggest keeping your daily cholesterol intake below **300 mg**, or **200 mg** if you're following a low cholesterol diet. To help you with this, each recipe in this book includes the cholesterol content, making it easy to keep track and stay within the recommended limits.

By knowing these numbers, you can enjoy tasty meals while managing your cholesterol and supporting your overall heart health.

Myths and Facts About Cholesterol

When it comes to cholesterol, there's a lot of confusion out there. Let's clear up some common myths and get to the facts.

Myth 1: If you're on cholesterol-lowering medication, you don't need to worry about your diet.
Fact: Even if you're taking medication to lower cholesterol, a healthy diet is still essential. Medications like statins help, but they work best when combined with heart-healthy eating. Relying solely on medication without making dietary changes can limit the overall benefits to your cholesterol levels and heart health.

Myth 2: You should avoid all fats to lower cholesterol.
Fact: Not all fats are created equal. Saturated and trans fats can raise your cholesterol, but healthy fats—like those from nuts, seeds, oily fish, and avocados—can actually help improve your cholesterol levels.

Myth 3: Only older people need to worry about cholesterol.
Fact: High cholesterol can affect anyone, even younger adults and children. It's a good idea to keep an eye on your cholesterol levels throughout your life.

Myth 4: You'll know if you have high cholesterol because you'll feel unwell.
Fact: High cholesterol doesn't usually have any symptoms, so the only way to know your levels is through a blood test. This is why regular check-ups are important.

Myth 5: If you're slim, you don't need to worry about cholesterol
Fact: Even if you're slim, you can still have high cholesterol. Cholesterol levels are influenced by many factors, including genetics, diet, and lifestyle, so it's important for everyone—regardless of size—to be mindful of their cholesterol.

By understanding the truth about cholesterol, you can make better choices for your heart health!

The Difference Between Good and Bad Cholesterol

Cholesterol is an essential part of your body's functioning, but not all cholesterol is the same. Understanding the difference between **'bad' cholesterol (LDL)** and **'good' cholesterol (HDL)** is key to managing your heart health.

Bad Cholesterol (LDL)

LDL, or low-density lipoprotein, is often referred to as 'bad' cholesterol. High levels of LDL can cause a build-up of plaque in the arteries, increasing the risk of heart disease and stroke. Keeping LDL levels low is important for protecting your heart.

HDL, or high-density lipoprotein, is known as 'good' cholesterol. It helps remove LDL from the bloodstream, transporting it to the liver where it can be broken down and eliminated from the body. Higher levels of HDL can reduce the risk of heart disease.

The Importance of Cholesterol Balance

Balancing LDL and HDL levels is crucial. While it's important to lower LDL, boosting your HDL levels can provide added protection for your heart.

Foods to Enjoy, Foods to Limit, and Foods to Avoid

When following a low cholesterol diet, it's essential to choose foods that lower LDL and raise HDL, while limiting those that may harm your cholesterol balance. Here's a guide to help you make the best choices for your heart.

Foods to Enjoy

These foods help maintain healthy cholesterol levels and support overall heart health:
- **Oats and Wholegrains (e.g., oats, barley, wholegrain bread):** Rich in soluble fibre, which helps lower LDL cholesterol by reducing its absorption in the bloodstream.
- **Oily Fish (e.g., salmon, mackerel, sardines):** High in omega-3 fatty acids, which lower LDL cholesterol and raise HDL levels for better heart health.
- **Nuts and Seeds (e.g., almonds, walnuts, flaxseeds):** Packed with healthy fats and fibre, which work together to improve cholesterol balance and support heart health.
- **Fruits (e.g., apples, pears, citrus fruits) and Vegetables (e.g., carrots, sweet potatoes, Brussels sprouts):** High in fibre and antioxidants, these help reduce cholesterol absorption and protect against heart disease.
- **Legumes (e.g., lentils, chickpeas):** A fantastic source of plant-based protein and fibre, which contribute to lowering LDL cholesterol.
- **Healthy Fats (e.g., olive oil, avocado):** These heart-healthy fats help raise HDL cholesterol while lowering LDL, supporting overall cholesterol balance.

Interesting Fact: it's generally okay to eat eggs on a low cholesterol diet for most people. In the past, eggs were thought to raise cholesterol levels because they contain dietary cholesterol. However, research now shows that saturated and trans fats in your diet have a much bigger effect on blood cholesterol than the cholesterol in eggs. Eggs are also a great source of protein and important nutrients, so there's no need to avoid them. If you're concerned, you can opt for egg whites or limit the number of yolks, but eggs can still fit into a heart-healthy diet.

Tip: Try incorporating these foods into your daily meals by swapping refined grains for wholegrains, adding nuts and seeds to salads or porridge, and using olive oil instead of butter in cooking.

Foods to Limit

Some foods should be eaten in moderation to avoid raising LDL levels:
- **Saturated Fats (e.g., fatty cuts of meat, full-fat dairy, butter):** These can raise LDL cholesterol and should be eaten in moderation.
- **Processed Meats (e.g., bacon, sausages, salami):** High in saturated fats, which can increase LDL cholesterol levels.
- **Fried Foods (e.g., fried chicken, chips, doughnuts):** Often cooked in unhealthy fats, leading to raised LDL cholesterol.

✓ **Tip:** Opt for lean cuts of meat like chicken, and use cooking methods like grilling, baking, or steaming instead of frying.

These foods can significantly raise LDL cholesterol and should be avoided or greatly reduced:

- **Trans Fats (e.g., processed foods like biscuits, pastries, margarine):** These unhealthy fats can raise LDL cholesterol and lower HDL, and should be avoided.
- **Fast Foods (e.g., burgers, fried chicken, chips):** Often loaded with unhealthy fats and high in calories, which contribute to high cholesterol levels.
- **Sugary Snacks (e.g., cakes, biscuits, doughnuts):** These frequently contain both saturated and trans fats, which negatively impact cholesterol levels.

✓ **Tip:** Always check food labels for saturated and trans fat content and opt for homemade versions of your favourite treats using healthier ingredients.

Reading Food Labels

When grocery shopping, reading food labels is essential. Look for products that are:

- **Low in Saturated Fat:** Aim for 3g or less per 100g.
- **Free of Trans Fats:** Avoid anything with 'hydrogenated' or 'partially hydrogenated' oils in the ingredients.
- **High in Fibre:** More fibre helps lower cholesterol by reducing its absorption in the body.

By focusing on foods that are good for your heart and limiting those that raise LDL cholesterol, you can make smart, heart-healthy choices. Remember to balance your diet, read labels carefully, and explore new ways to enjoy the delicious foods that support better cholesterol levels and overall wellbeing.

Cholesterol Levels for Adults and Children

Understanding healthy cholesterol levels is key to maintaining heart health for both adults and children. Cholesterol is measured in millimoles per litre (mmol/L) in the UK, and the levels can vary depending on age, lifestyle, and overall health.

Cholesterol Levels for Adults

For adults, a healthy cholesterol level helps reduce the risk of heart disease and stroke. Here are the general guidelines for total cholesterol and its types:

- **Total cholesterol:** 5 mmol/L or below is considered healthy.
- **LDL (bad cholesterol):** 3 mmol/L or lower is ideal.
- **HDL (good cholesterol):** 1 mmol/L or higher is recommended for heart health.
- **Non-HDL cholesterol (total cholesterol minus HDL):** 4 mmol/L or lower is considered healthy.

Regular cholesterol checks with your GP are important, especially if you have risk factors such as a family history of heart disease or high cholesterol.

Cholesterol Levels for Children

While children generally have lower cholesterol levels than adults, high cholesterol can still be a concern, especially for those with a family history of heart issues. Here are the typical cholesterol ranges for children:

- **Total cholesterol:** Below 4.5 mmol/L is considered healthy for children.

- **LDL (bad cholesterol):** Below 3 mmol/L is recommended for children.

Encouraging children to eat a balanced diet with plenty of fruits, vegetables, wholegrains, and healthy fats can help maintain good cholesterol levels from a young age.

Keeping Cholesterol in Check

Whether for adults or children, a healthy lifestyle with a balanced diet, regular exercise, and avoiding smoking can help maintain good cholesterol levels and support long-term heart health.

Chapter 2: 31-Day Low Cholesterol Meal Plan

Transitioning to a low-cholesterol diet can be a rewarding journey, full of vibrant flavours, balanced meals, and nourishing ingredients. This 31-day meal plan has been designed to include breakfast, lunch, dinner, snacks, desserts, and smoothies, ensuring each day feels satisfying and varied. The plan is flexible, allowing you to swap in other recipes from this book to suit your preferences or schedule, keeping your meals both interesting and easy to prepare.

Week 1: Building a Flavourful Foundation

Start the journey with a variety of wholesome and flavour-packed dishes to kickstart your healthier lifestyle.

Day 1
- **Breakfast**: Wholegrain Avocado and Tomato Toast
- **Lunch**: Sweet Potato and Leek Broth
- **Dinner**: Grilled Salmon with Lemon and Dill, Spinach and Orange Salad with Walnuts
- **Snack**: Apple Slices with Nut Butter
- **Dessert**: Dark Chocolate and Orange Mousse
- **Smoothie**: Green Goodness Kiwi and Spinach Smoothie

Day 2
- **Breakfast**: Cinnamon and Raisin Porridge with Almond Milk
- **Lunch**: Classic Minestrone with Wholegrain Pasta
- **Dinner**: Lemon and Herb Baked Turkey Breast, Roasted Brussels Sprouts with Balsamic Glaze
- **Snack**: Cucumber and Avocado Bites
- **Dessert**: Raspberry and Almond Yoghurt Pots
- **Smoothie**: Pineapple and Kale Immune Booster

Day 3
- **Breakfast**: Toasted Rye Bread with Smashed Peas and Mint
- **Lunch**: Broccoli and Spinach Detox Soup
- **Dinner**: Baked Haddock with a Light Mustard Glaze, Herbed Brown Rice with Peas
- **Snack**: Crispy Roasted Chickpeas with Spices
- **Dessert**: Banana and Date Loaf
- **Smoothie**: Beetroot and Berry Antioxidant Shake

Day 4
- **Breakfast**: Low-Fat Greek Yoghurt with Honey and Flaxseeds

- **Lunch**: Herby Mushroom and Sweet Potato Broth
- **Dinner**: Chicken and Spinach Curry
- **Snack**: Courgette Chips with Herbs
- **Dessert**: Apple and Cinnamon Oat Crumble
- **Smoothie**: Peach and Chia Seed Hydration Smoothie

Day 5
- **Breakfast**: Muesli with Nuts, Seeds, and Fresh Fruit
- **Lunch**: Spiced Carrot and Ginger Soup
- **Dinner**: Grilled Lamb Chops with Mint Yoghurt Sauce, Roasted Carrots with Thyme and Olive Oil
- **Snack**: Roasted Cauliflower Bites with Garlic Dip
- **Dessert**: Low-Cholesterol Victoria Sponge Cake
- **Smoothie**: Carrot and Orange Vitamin Boost Smoothie

Day 6
- **Breakfast**: Overnight Oats with Apple and Cinnamon
- **Lunch**: Chickpea and Spinach Stew
- **Dinner**: Baked Sea Bass with Lemon and Rocket, Courgette Ribbons with Lemon and Pine Nuts
- **Snack**: Smashed Avocado and Tomato Bruschetta
- **Dessert**: Strawberry and Basil Sorbet
- **Smoothie**: Banana, Date, and Cinnamon Smoothie

Day 7
- **Breakfast**: Smoothie Bowl with Oats, Flaxseeds, and Fruits
- **Lunch**: Spiced Prawn and Vegetable Stew
- **Dinner**: Mediterranean Chicken Bake with Olives and Tomatoes, Tomato, Cucumber, and Mint Salad
- **Snack**: Oven-Baked Falafel Balls
- **Dessert**: Blueberry and Lemon Drizzle Traybake
- **Smoothie**: Cucumber, Celery, and Apple Cleanse Smoothie

Week 2: Expanding Your Palate

Explore bolder flavours and creative low-cholesterol meal ideas.

Day 8
- **Breakfast**: Scrambled Eggs with Spinach and Mushrooms
- **Lunch**: Roasted Cauliflower with Tahini Dressing
- **Dinner**: Stuffed Chicken Breast with Garlic and Spinach
- **Snack**: Herbed Wholemeal Pitta Bread with Baba Ganoush
- **Dessert**: Spiced Poached Pears with a Hint of Ginger
- **Smoothie**: Blueberry and Flaxseed Power Shake

Day 9
- **Breakfast**: Spiced Lentil Porridge with a Twist
- **Lunch**: Cabbage and White Bean Soup
- **Dinner**: Steamed Salmon and Broccoli with Ginger and Soy Sauce
- **Snack**: Stuffed Tomatoes with Quinoa
- **Dessert**: Peach and Passionfruit Eton Mess
- **Smoothie**: Creamy Avocado and Lime Smoothie

Day 10
- **Breakfast**: Egg White Omelette with Peppers and Onion

- **Lunch**: Chickpea and Spinach Curry
- **Dinner**: Baked Pork Fillet with Herbs, Green Bean Salad with Dijon Mustard Vinaigrette
- **Snack**: Crispy Roasted Chickpeas with Spices
- **Dessert**: Vanilla Rice Pudding with Berry Compote
- **Smoothie**: Pineapple and Turmeric Anti-Inflammatory Smoothie

Day 11
- **Breakfast**: Oat and Banana Pancakes with Fresh Fruit
- **Lunch**: Butternut Squash and Coconut Stew
- **Dinner**: Seared Tuna with a Sesame Crust, Grilled Asparagus with Lemon and Olive Oil
- **Snack**: Cucumber Rounds with Tzatziki
- **Dessert**: Apricot and Pistachio Energy Bites
- **Smoothie**: Strawberry and Basil Detox Blend

Day 12
- **Breakfast**: Grilled Tomatoes and Mushrooms on Toast
- **Lunch**: Lemon and Lentil Soup
- **Dinner**: Spicy Chicken and Sweet Potato Bake, Cabbage and Carrot Coleslaw with Greek Yoghurt Dressing
- **Snack**: Baked Beetroot Crisps
- **Dessert**: Honey and Oat Flapjacks
- **Smoothie**: Cherry and Almond Energy Smoothie

Day 13
- **Breakfast**: Smoothie Bowl with Banana, Date, and Cinnamon Smoothie
- **Lunch**: Chicken and Vegetable Barley Stew
- **Dinner**: Mediterranean Lamb Meatballs with Tomato Sauce, Roasted Brussels Sprouts with Balsamic Glaze
- **Snack**: Chicken and Vegetable Lettuce Wraps
- **Dessert**: Baked Plums with Cinnamon and Maple Syrup
- **Smoothie**: Pineapple and Kale Immune Booster

Day 14
- **Breakfast**: Muesli with Nuts, Seeds, and Fresh Fruit
- **Lunch**: Broccoli and Almond Slaw
- **Dinner**: Stuffed Sweet Peppers with Quinoa and Black Beans
- **Snack**: Oven-Baked Falafel Balls
- **Dessert**: Chilled Mango and Coconut Rice Pudding
- **Smoothie**: Beetroot and Berry Antioxidant Shake

Week 3: Revitalising Your Routine

Reinvigorate your meals with fresh, exciting combinations that bring balance and joy to your low-cholesterol journey.

Day 15
- **Breakfast**: Wholegrain Avocado and Tomato Toast
- **Lunch**: Mushroom and Barley Broth
- **Dinner**: Herb-Crusted Fillet Steak with Mustard Sauce, Grilled Asparagus with Lemon and Olive Oil
- **Snack**: Herbed Wholemeal Pitta Bread with Baba Ganoush
- **Dessert**: Low-Cholesterol Victoria Sponge Cake
- **Smoothie**: Berry and Oat Breakfast Smoothie

Day 16
- **Breakfast**: Muesli with Nuts, Seeds, and Fresh Fruit
- **Lunch**: Broccoli and Spinach Detox Soup
- **Dinner**: Spicy Quinoa and Black Bean Burger, Tomato, Cucumber, and Mint Salad
- **Snack**: Courgette Chips with Herbs
- **Dessert**: Raspberry and Almond Yoghurt Pots
- **Smoothie**: Cucumber, Celery, and Apple Cleanse Smoothie

Day 17
- **Breakfast**: Scrambled Eggs with Spinach and Mushrooms
- **Lunch**: Lemon and Lentil Soup
- **Dinner**: Grilled Chicken Skewers with Herbs, Roasted Sweet Potato Wedges with Spices
- **Snack**: Stuffed Tomatoes with Quinoa
- **Dessert**: Dark Chocolate and Orange Mousse
- **Smoothie**: Green Goodness Kiwi and Spinach Smoothie

Day 18
- **Breakfast**: Egg White Omelette with Peppers and Onion
- **Lunch**: Cabbage and White Bean Soup
- **Dinner**: Oven-Baked Chicken with Tomatoes and Basil, Roasted Carrots with Thyme and Olive Oil
- **Snack**: Roasted Cauliflower Bites with Garlic Dip
- **Dessert**: Apple and Cinnamon Oat Crumble
- **Smoothie**: Peach and Chia Seed Hydration Smoothie

Day 19
- **Breakfast**: Baked Beans on Wholemeal Toast
- **Lunch**: Spiced Prawn and Vegetable Stew
- **Dinner**: Baked Salmon with Oranges, Lemons, and Herb Blend, Courgette Ribbons with Lemon and Pine Nuts
- **Snack**: Smashed Avocado and Tomato Bruschetta
- **Dessert**: Blueberry and Lemon Drizzle Traybake
- **Smoothie**: Cherry and Almond Energy Smoothie

Day 20
- **Breakfast**: Smoothie Bowl with Oats, Flaxseeds, and Fruits
- **Lunch**: Classic Minestrone with Wholegrain Pasta
- **Dinner**: Chicken and Vegetable Bake, Broccoli and Almond Slaw
- **Snack**: Chicken and Vegetable Lettuce Wraps
- **Dessert**: Spiced Poached Pears with a Hint of Ginger
- **Smoothie**: Pineapple and Turmeric Anti-Inflammatory Smoothie

Day 21
- **Breakfast**: Overnight Oats with Apple and Cinnamon
- **Lunch**: Herby Mushroom and Sweet Potato Broth
- **Dinner**: Mediterranean Vegetable and Cod Casserole, Roasted Brussels Sprouts with Balsamic Glaze
- **Snack**: Crispy Roasted Chickpeas with Spices
- **Dessert**: Vanilla Rice Pudding with Berry Compote
- **Smoothie**: Carrot and Orange Vitamin Boost Smoothie

Week 4: Refining Your Habits

Focus on wholesome and satisfying meals that support your healthy lifestyle while keeping flavours vibrant and indulgent.

Day 22
- **Breakfast**: Oat and Banana Pancakes with Fresh Fruit
- **Lunch**: Butternut Squash and Coconut Stew
- **Dinner**: Grilled Lamb Chops with Mint Yoghurt Sauce, Spinach and Orange Salad with Walnuts
- **Snack**: Herbed Wholemeal Pitta Bread with Baba Ganoush
- **Dessert**: Low-Cholesterol Victoria Sponge Cake
- **Smoothie**: Beetroot and Berry Antioxidant Shake

Day 23
- **Breakfast**: Grilled Tomatoes and Mushrooms on Toast
- **Lunch**: Chickpea and Spinach Curry
- **Dinner**: Lemon and Herb Pasta with Grilled Prawns, Roasted Brussels Sprouts with Balsamic Glaze
- **Snack**: Stuffed Tomatoes with Quinoa
- **Dessert**: Baked Plums with Cinnamon and Maple Syrup
- **Smoothie**: Creamy Avocado and Lime Smoothie

Day 24
- **Breakfast**: Low-Fat Greek Yoghurt with Honey and Flaxseeds
- **Lunch**: Cabbage and White Bean Soup
- **Dinner**: Baked Beef and Vegetable Casserole, Roasted Cauliflower with Tahini Dressing
- **Snack**: Courgette Chips with Herbs
- **Dessert**: Raspberry and Almond Yoghurt Pots
- **Smoothie**: Berry and Oat Breakfast Smoothie

Day 25
- **Breakfast**: Wholegrain Avocado and Tomato Toast
- **Lunch**: Broccoli and Spinach Detox Soup
- **Dinner**: Stuffed Chicken Breast with Garlic and Spinach, Sweet Potato Wedges with Spices
- **Snack**: Smashed Avocado and Tomato Bruschetta
- **Dessert**: Blueberry and Lemon Drizzle Traybake
- **Smoothie**: Cucumber, Celery, and Apple Cleanse Smoothie

Day 26
- **Breakfast**: Cinnamon and Raisin Porridge with Almond Milk
- **Lunch**: Spiced Carrot and Ginger Soup
- **Dinner**: Steamed Beef and Vegetable Dumplings, Tomato, Cucumber, and Mint Salad
- **Snack**: Cucumber and Avocado Bites
- **Dessert**: Honey and Oat Flapjacks
- **Smoothie**: Green Goodness Kiwi and Spinach Smoothie

Day 27
- **Breakfast**: Scrambled Eggs with Spinach and Mushrooms
- **Lunch**: Chickpea and Spinach Stew
- **Dinner**: Herb-Crusted Lamb Cutlets, Roasted Brussels Sprouts with Balsamic Glaze
- **Snack**: Roasted Cauliflower Bites with Garlic Dip
- **Dessert**: Chilled Mango and Coconut Rice Pudding
- **Smoothie**: Pineapple and Kale Immune Booster

Day 28
- **Breakfast**: Muesli with Nuts, Seeds, and Fresh Fruit
- **Lunch**: Herby Mushroom and Sweet Potato Broth
- **Dinner**: Steamed Chicken with Ginger and Broccoli, Green Bean Salad with Dijon Mustard Vinaigrette
- **Snack**: Crispy Roasted Chickpeas with Spices
- **Dessert**: Apricot and Pistachio Energy Bites

- **Smoothie**: Banana, Date, and Cinnamon Smoothie

Week 5: Mastering a Healthy Lifestyle

Finish the month strong with creative, heart-healthy dishes that celebrate everything you've learned on your low-cholesterol journey.

Day 29
- **Breakfast**: Egg White Omelette with Peppers and Onion
- **Lunch**: Mushroom Stroganoff with Wholegrain Pasta
- **Dinner**: Herb-Crusted Baked Haddock, Courgette Ribbons with Lemon and Pine Nuts
- **Snack**: Stuffed Tomatoes with Quinoa
- **Dessert**: Dark Chocolate and Orange Mousse
- **Smoothie**: Cherry and Almond Energy Smoothie

Day 30
- **Breakfast**: Oat and Banana Pancakes with Fresh Fruit
- **Lunch**: Sweet Potato and Leek Broth
- **Dinner**: Baked Flank Steak with Garlic and Rosemary, Roasted Brussels Sprouts with Balsamic Glaze
- **Snack**: Cucumber and Avocado Bites
- **Dessert**: Vanilla Rice Pudding with Berry Compote
- **Smoothie**: Strawberry and Basil Detox Blend

Day 31
- **Breakfast**: Wholegrain Avocado and Tomato Toast
- **Lunch**: Chicken and Spinach Stew
- **Dinner**: Baked Sea Bass with Lemon and Rocket, Grilled Asparagus with Lemon and Olive Oil
- **Snack**: Smashed Avocado and Tomato Bruschetta
- **Dessert**: Peach and Passionfruit Eton Mess
- **Smoothie**: Pineapple and Turmeric Anti-Inflammatory Smoothie

Chapter 3: Recipes for a Heart-Healthy Lifestyle

Dive into this chapter for a comprehensive collection of low-cholesterol recipes designed to keep your meals both delicious and nutritious. From hearty mains and vibrant salads to refreshing smoothies and flavour-packed sauces, every recipe is crafted to support your health without compromising on taste. Whether you're planning breakfast, lunch, dinner, or snacks, you'll find something here to suit your lifestyle and palate.

Breakfast

Why Breakfast Matters for a Low Cholesterol Diet
A healthy breakfast sets the tone for your day. It provides the energy you need to get started and keeps you feeling full until lunchtime. For a low cholesterol lifestyle, breakfast is the perfect opportunity to incorporate fibre-rich whole grains, healthy fats, and plant-based proteins to support heart health and maintain balanced cholesterol levels.

What to Include in a Low Cholesterol Breakfast
- **Whole Grains:** Oats, wholegrain bread, or rye offer soluble fibre, which can help reduce cholesterol absorption.
- **Healthy Fats:** Foods like avocado, seeds, and nuts provide essential fats to support your heart.
- **Fruits and Vegetables:** Add berries, bananas, tomatoes, or leafy greens for a boost of vitamins and antioxidants.
- **Plant-Based Proteins:** Incorporate nut butters, seeds, or legumes for a satisfying start.

Tips for Breakfast Success
- Choose unsweetened plant-based milks (like almond, oat, or soya milk) over full-fat dairy.
- Use natural sweeteners like honey or maple syrup sparingly.
- Experiment with fresh herbs, spices, and citrus for extra flavour without adding salt or sugar.

With these nourishing recipes, your mornings will become a time to enjoy delicious, healthful dishes while working towards your cholesterol-lowering goals.

Some of these recipes can be prepared the night before, so you're never too rushed in the morning.

If you're still feeling hungry, pair your breakfast with a quick salad: toss together some leafy greens, avocado, nuts, and a drizzle of olive oil for a heart-healthy boost!

Enjoy trying these tasty and easy-to-make breakfast ideas as you begin your day with a healthy mindset!

Scrambled Eggs with Spinach and Mushrooms

Preparation Time: 5 minutes | **Cooking Time:** 10 minutes | **Servings:** 1

Ingredients:
2 large egg whites (or 1 whole egg + 1 egg white)
2 teaspoons olive oil
50 g fresh spinach
50 g mushrooms, sliced
½ small onion, finely chopped)
1 teaspoon semi-skimmed milk or plant-based milk
½ teaspoon plant-based spread (optional)
Pinch of salt and pepper
Fresh parsley or chives (optional)

Instructions:
1. Heat 2 teaspoons of olive oil in a pan over medium heat. Add the onion and cook for 2-3 minutes until soft. Add mushrooms and sauté for 4-5 minutes until tender, then stir in the spinach until wilted. Set aside.
2. In a bowl, whisk the egg whites (or egg mixture) with milk, salt, and pepper.
3. In the same pan, add plant-based spread if using, then pour in the egg mixture. Cook gently, stirring for 2-3 minutes until scrambled and creamy.
4. Fold in the cooked spinach and mushrooms, and garnish with parsley or chives if desired.

Serving Suggestions:
Add a slice of wholegrain toast or a quick salad with leafy greens, avocado, and a drizzle of olive oil for a heart-healthy meal.

Nutritional Information (Per Serving):
Calories: 85 kcal | Total Fat: 4 g (Saturated Fat: 0.8g) | Cholesterol: 3 mg (with egg whites only, 45 mg with yolk) | Fibre: 1.5 g | Protein: 6.5 g

Overnight Oats with Apple and Cinnamon

Preparation Time: 5 minutes | **Chill Time:** 4-8 hours (overnight) | **Serves:** 1

Ingredients:
40 g rolled oats
100 ml semi-skimmed milk or plant-based milk (fortified with sterols)
½ apple, grated or finely chopped (around 50 g)
1 tablespoon chia seeds (optional, for extra fibre)
¼ teaspoon ground cinnamon
1 teaspoon honey or maple syrup (optional)
1 tablespoon plain low-fat yoghurt (optional, for creaminess)

Instructions:
1. In a jar or bowl, combine the oats, milk, chia seeds (if using), cinnamon, and honey or syrup if desired. Stir well to mix everything evenly.
2. Add the grated or chopped apple and mix again. Cover the jar or bowl and place it in the fridge for at least 4 hours, preferably overnight.
3. In the morning, stir the oats, top with a spoonful of yoghurt (if using), and add an extra sprinkle of cinnamon for garnish if desired.

Serving Suggestions:
For added crunch and heart-healthy fats, top your oats with a handful of chopped nuts or seeds in the morning. Serve with a side of fresh berries for extra fibre and antioxidants.

Nutritional Information (Per Serving):
Calories: 200 kcal | Total Fat: 5 g (Saturated Fat: 1 g) | Cholesterol: 0 mg | Fibre: 6 g | Protein: 6 g.

Baked Beans on Wholemeal Toast

Preparation Time: 5 minutes | **Cooking Time:** 5-7 minutes | **Servings:** 1

Ingredients:
½ can (200 g) reduced-sugar, reduced-salt baked beans
1 slice wholemeal bread
1 teaspoon olive oil (optional, for toasting)
Pinch of black pepper
Fresh parsley (optional, for garnish)

Instructions:
1. Heat 2 teaspoons of olive oil in a pan over medium heat. Add the Heat the baked beans in a pan over medium heat for 3-5 minutes, stirring occasionally until warmed through.
2. Toast the wholemeal bread while the beans are heating. For extra flavour, you can brush the bread with olive oil before toasting.
3. Serve the hot baked beans on top of the toast, season with black pepper, and garnish with fresh parsley if desired.

Serving Suggestions:
Pair with grilled tomatoes or a side of leafy greens with a drizzle of olive oil to boost the heart-healthy benefits.

Nutritional Information (Per Serving):
Calories: 250 kcal | Total Fat: 5 g (Saturated Fat: 0.8 g) | Cholesterol: 0 mg | Fibre: 8 g | Protein: 10 g

Oat and Banana Pancakes with Fresh Fruit

Preparation Time: 5 minutes | **Cooking Time:** 10 minutes | **Servings:** 1

Ingredients:
40 g rolled oats
1 ripe banana (about 100 g)
1 large egg white (or 1 whole egg)
1 teaspoon baking powder (optional)
1 teaspoon cinnamon (optional)
1 teaspoon olive oil (for cooking)
Fresh fruit, such as berries or sliced apples, for topping
1 teaspoon honey or maple syrup (optional)

Instructions:
1. In a blender, combine the oats, banana, egg white (or whole egg), baking powder, and cinnamon if using. Blend until smooth.
2. Heat the olive oil in a pan over medium heat. Pour in small portions of the batter to form pancakes. Cook for 2-3 minutes on each side, or until golden and cooked through.
3. Serve the pancakes topped with fresh fruit and drizzle with honey or syrup if desired.

Serving Suggestions:
Serve with a side of Greek yoghurt or add a handful of nuts for an extra boost of protein and heart-healthy fats.

Nutritional Information (Per Serving):
Calories: 220 kcal | Total Fat: 7g (Saturated Fat: 1 g) | Cholesterol: 0 mg (with egg white, 55mg with whole egg) | Fibre: 5 g | Protein: 7 g

Egg White Omelette with Peppers and Onion

Preparation Time: 5 minutes | **Cooking Time:** 5-7 minutes | **Servings:** 1

Ingredients:
3 large egg whites
1 teaspoon olive oil (5 ml)
½ small onion, finely chopped
(about 25 g)
½ red or green pepper, diced (about
50 g)
Pinch of salt and black pepper
Fresh parsley or chives (optional,
for garnish)

Instructions:
1. Heat the olive oil in a pan over medium heat. Add the onion and pepper, cooking for 3-4 minutes until softened.
2. In a bowl, whisk the egg whites with a pinch of salt and pepper.
3. Pour the egg whites over the vegetables in the pan and cook gently for 2-3 minutes, or until the egg whites are set. Fold the omelette in half.
4. Garnish with fresh parsley or chives if desired and serve.

Serving Suggestions:
Serve with a slice of wholegrain toast or a side of grilled tomatoes for added fibre and heart-healthy benefits.

Nutritional Information (Per Serving):
Calories: 90 kcal | Total Fat: 4 g (Saturated Fat: 0.5 g) | Cholesterol: 0 mg | Fibre: 2 g | Protein: 9 g

Muesli with Nuts, Seeds, and Fresh Fruit

Preparation Time: 5 minutes | **Servings:** 1

Ingredients:
40 g rolled oats
1 tablespoon mixed nuts (e.g., almonds, walnuts)
1 tablespoon mixed seeds (e.g., chia seeds, flaxseeds)
100ml semi-skimmed milk or plant-based milk (fortified with sterols)
1 small apple or banana, chopped
1 teaspoon honey or maple syrup (optional)

Instructions:
1. In a bowl, combine the rolled oats, nuts, and seeds.
2. Pour the milk over the muesli mixture and stir to combine.
3. Top with the chopped fruit and drizzle with honey or maple syrup if desired.

Serving Suggestions:
Serve with a side of Greek yoghurt or add a handful of nuts for an extra boost of protein and heart-healthy fats.

Nutritional Information (Per Serving):
Calories: 280 kcal | Total Fat: 12g (Saturated Fat: 1.5 g) | Cholesterol: 0 mg | Fibre: 7 g | Protein: 8 g

Wholegrain Avocado and Tomato Toast

Preparation Time: 5 minutes | **Cooking Time:** 5 minutes | **Servings:** 1

Ingredients:
1 slice wholegrain bread
½ ripe avocado (about 60 g), mashed
1 medium tomato, sliced
1 teaspoon olive oil (optional)
Pinch of salt and black pepper
Squeeze of fresh lemon juice (optional)
Fresh basil or parsley for garnish (optional)

Instructions:
1. Toast the slice of wholegrain bread until golden brown.
2. Mash the avocado in a small bowl and season with a pinch of salt, black pepper, and a squeeze of fresh lemon juice if desired.
3. Spread the mashed avocado evenly over the toast. Top with sliced tomato, drizzle with olive oil (if using), and season with additional salt and pepper.
4. Garnish with fresh basil or parsley if desired and serve immediately.

Serving Suggestions:
For added protein, pair with a poached egg or enjoy with a side of fresh fruit for a balanced and heart-healthy breakfast.

Tip:
To cook a perfect poached egg, bring a small pot of water to a gentle simmer and add a splash of vinegar (optional, to help the egg hold its shape). Crack the egg into a small bowl, then gently slide it into the simmering water. Cook for about 3 minutes until the whites are set but the yolk is still runny. Remove with a slotted spoon and serve immediately.

Nutritional Information (Per Serving):
Calories: 220 kcal | Total Fat: 15 g (Saturated Fat: 2 g) | Cholesterol: 0 mg | Fibre: 6 g | Protein: 5 g

Low-Fat Greek Yoghurt with Honey and Flaxseeds

Preparation Time: 2 minutes | **Servings:** 1

Ingredients:
40 g rolled oats
150 g low-fat Greek yoghurt
1 teaspoon honey
1 tablespoon flaxseeds
Fresh berries or sliced fruit (optional)

Instructions:
1. Spoon the low-fat Greek yoghurt into a bowl.
2. Drizzle the honey over the yoghurt.
3. Sprinkle with flaxseeds for added fibre and healthy fats.
4. Add fresh berries or sliced fruit if desired and serve immediately.

Serving Suggestions:
For a protein boost, pair this yoghurt with a handful of nuts or seeds, or serve alongside wholegrain toast for a more filling breakfast.

Nutritional Information (Per Serving):
Calories: 180 kcal | Total Fat: 5 g (Saturated Fat: 1 g) | Cholesterol: 5 mg | Fibre: 4 g | Protein: 12 g

Toasted Rye Bread with Smashed Peas and Mint

Preparation Time: 5 minutes | **Cooking Time:** 5 minutes | **Servings:** 1

Ingredients:
1 slice rye bread
80 g frozen peas
1 teaspoon olive oil
1 tablespoon fresh mint leaves, chopped
1 teaspoon lemon juice
Pinch of salt and black pepper
Fresh mint leaves for garnish (optional)

Instructions:
1. Toast the rye bread until golden brown.
2. Cook the peas by bringing a small pot of water to a rolling boil. Add the peas to the boiling water and cook for 2-3 minutes until tender. Drain the peas and transfer them to a small bowl. (You can also cook the peas the evening before and refrigerate them until ready to use.)
3. Smash the peas with a fork, stirring in the olive oil, chopped mint, lemon juice, and a pinch of salt and pepper until combined.
4. Spread the smashed peas over the toasted rye bread. Garnish with extra mint leaves if desired, and serve immediately

Serving Suggestions:
For added flavour, crumble a small amount of feta cheese on top. Feta is lower in fat than many cheeses, but it still contains some saturated fat, so enjoy it in moderation. You can also pair the toast with a poached egg for extra protein or serve with a fresh tomato salad for a balanced, heart-healthy meal.

Tip:
To cook a perfect poached egg, bring a small pot of water to a gentle simmer and add a splash of vinegar (optional, to help the egg hold its shape). Crack the egg into a small bowl, then gently slide it into the simmering water. Cook for about 3 minutes until the whites are set but the yolk is still runny. Remove with a slotted spoon and serve immediately.

Nutritional Information (Per Serving):
Calories: 180 kcal | Total Fat: 6 g (Saturated Fat: 0.8 g) | Cholesterol: 0 mg | Fibre: 7 g | Protein: 7 g

Spiced Lentil Porridge with a Twist

Preparation Time: 5 minutes | **Cooking Time:** 20 minutes | **Servings:** 1

Ingredients:
50 g red lentils, rinsed
250 ml water or low-sodium vegetable stock (available in most supermarkets or health food shops, or homemade to control salt)
¼ teaspoon ground cumin
¼ teaspoon ground turmeric
Pinch of ground cinnamon
1 teaspoon olive oil
1 small clove garlic, minced (optional)
1 tablespoon plain low-fat yoghurt (optional)
Fresh coriander leaves for garnish

Instructions:
1. Cook the lentils by bringing the rinsed lentils and water or vegetable stock to a boil in a small pot. Reduce the heat and simmer gently for 15-20 minutes until the lentils are soft and most of the liquid is absorbed. (You can cook the lentils the evening before and refrigerate them until ready to use.)
2. Stir in the cumin, turmeric, and cinnamon, along with the olive oil. Add the minced garlic if using, and season with salt and pepper to taste. Cook for another 2-3 minutes to blend the flavours.
3. Spoon the lentil porridge into a bowl. Top with a dollop of plain low-fat yoghurt and garnish with fresh coriander leaves if desired.

Serving Suggestions:
For a heartier meal, pair with a slice of wholegrain toast or top with roasted vegetables for added texture and flavour.

Nutritional Information (Per Serving):
Calories: 220 kcal | Total Fat: 6 g (Saturated Fat: 1 g) | Cholesterol: 0 mg | Fibre: 8 g | Protein: 12 g

Cinnamon and Raisin Porridge with Almond Milk

Preparation Time: 5 minutes | **Cooking Time:** 5-7 minutes | **Servings:** 1

Ingredients:
40 g rolled oats
250 ml unsweetened almond milk
1 tablespoon raisins
½ teaspoon ground cinnamon
1 teaspoon honey or maple syrup (optional)
Pinch of salt
Fresh fruit or nuts for topping (optional)

Instructions:
1. In a small pot, combine the oats, almond milk, raisins, cinnamon, and a pinch of salt.
2. Bring the mixture to a gentle simmer over medium heat, stirring occasionally, and cook for 5-7 minutes until the oats are soft and the porridge has thickened.
3. Remove from heat and stir in honey or maple syrup if desired. Serve immediately, topped with fresh fruit or nuts for extra flavour and texture.

Serving Suggestions:
Add a handful of chopped nuts or seeds for extra crunch, or top with sliced banana or fresh berries for a naturally sweet and fibre-rich addition.

Nutritional Information (Per Serving):
Calories: 200 kcal | Total Fat: 4 g (Saturated Fat: 0.3 g) | Cholesterol: 0 mg | Fibre: 4 g | Protein: 5 g

Grilled Tomatoes and Mushrooms on Toast

Preparation Time: 5 minutes | **Cooking Time:** 10 minutes | **Servings:** 1

Ingredients:
1 slice wholegrain bread
1 medium tomato, halved
50 g mushrooms, sliced
1 teaspoon olive oil
½ teaspoon balsamic vinegar (optional)
Pinch of salt and black pepper
Fresh parsley or basil for garnish (optional)

Instructions:
1. Heat the grill to medium. Place the tomato halves and sliced mushrooms on a baking tray. Drizzle with olive oil and season with salt and pepper.
2. Grill for 5-7 minutes until the tomatoes are softened and slightly charred, and the mushrooms are golden.
3. While the vegetables are grilling, toast the wholegrain bread.
4. Once the vegetables are done, place them on the toast. Drizzle with balsamic vinegar if desired, and garnish with fresh parsley or basil. Serve immediately.

Serving Suggestions:
Pair with a poached egg for added protein, or add a side of avocado for a boost of healthy fats and extra creaminess.

Tip:
To cook a perfect poached egg, bring a small pot of water to a gentle simmer and add a splash of vinegar (optional, to help the egg hold its shape). Crack the egg into a small bowl, then gently slide it into the simmering water. Cook for about 3 minutes until the whites are set but the yolk is still runny. Remove with a slotted spoon and serve immediately.

Nutritional Information (Per Serving):
Calories: 180 kcal | Total Fat: 7 g (Saturated Fat: 1 g) | Cholesterol: 0 mg | Fibre: 5 g | Protein: 5 g

Smoothie Bowl with Oats, Flaxseeds, and Fruits

Preparation Time: 5 minutes | **Servings:** 1

Ingredients:
30 g rolled oats
1 tablespoon flaxseeds
1 small banana, sliced
100 g mixed berries (e.g., strawberries, blueberries)
150 ml unsweetened almond milk or other plant-based milk
1 teaspoon honey or maple syrup (optional)
Fresh fruit, nuts, or seeds for topping (optional)

Instructions:
1. In a blender, combine the oats, flaxseeds, banana, mixed berries, and almond milk. Blend until smooth and creamy.
2. Pour the smoothie into a bowl. Drizzle with honey or maple syrup if desired.
3. Top with additional fresh fruit, nuts, or seeds for extra texture and nutrients. Serve immediately.

Serving Suggestions:
Top with sliced kiwi, chia seeds, or a handful of granola for added crunch and nutrients.

Nutritional Information (Per Serving):
Calories: 250 kcal | Total Fat: 7 g (Saturated Fat: 0.5 g) | Cholesterol: 0 mg | Fibre: 8 g | Protein: 6 g

Avocado and Hummus on Rye Toast

Preparation Time: 5 minutes | **Servings:** 1

Ingredients:
1 slice rye bread
½ ripe avocado (about 60 g), mashed
2 tablespoons hummus
1 teaspoon lemon juice
Pinch of salt and black pepper
Fresh parsley or chilli flakes for garnish (optional)

Instructions:
1. Toast the slice of rye bread until golden brown.
2. In a small bowl, mash the avocado with the lemon juice, and season with a pinch of salt and black pepper.
3. Spread the hummus evenly over the toasted rye bread.
4. Top with the mashed avocado, garnish with fresh parsley or chilli flakes if desired, and serve immediately.

Serving Suggestions:
Pair with a side of cherry tomatoes or a simple green salad for added freshness and fibre.

Nutritional Information (Per Serving):
Calories: 220 kcal | Total Fat: 14 g (Saturated Fat: 2 g) | Cholesterol: 0 mg | Fibre: 7 g | Protein: 5 g

Chickpea Pancake with Herbs

Preparation Time: 5 minutes | **Cooking Time:** 5 minutes | **Servings:** 1

Ingredients:
50 g chickpea flour (gram flour)
75 ml water
½ tablespoon olive oil, plus extra for cooking
½ spring onion, finely chopped
1 small handful of fresh parsley or coriander, chopped
¼ teaspoon ground cumin
A pinch of turmeric
Salt and black pepper to taste

Instructions:
1. In a small bowl, whisk the chickpea flour with water, olive oil, cumin, turmeric, salt, and black pepper until you have a smooth batter. Stir in the chopped spring onion and herbs.
2. Heat a drizzle of olive oil in a small frying pan over medium heat. Pour in the batter, swirling the pan to spread it into a thin pancake.
3. Cook for 3–4 minutes until the edges are set and the bottom is golden brown. Flip and cook for another 2–3 minutes.
4. Serve the pancake warm, with a fresh side salad or a dollop of tomato chutney if desired.
5.

Serving Suggestions:
Mash half an avocado with lime juice, salt, and a touch of chilli flakes. Spread it over the pancake or serve as a dip.

Nutritional Information (Per Serving):
Calories: 190 kcal | Total Fat: 7 g (Saturated Fat: 1 g) | Cholesterol: 0 mg | Fibre: 4 g | Protein: 7 g

Sweet Potato and Spinach Hash

Preparation Time: 10 minutes | **Cooking Time:** 15 minutes | **Servings:** 1

Ingredients:
100 g sweet potato, peeled and diced
½ small red onion, finely chopped
½ red pepper, diced
1 handful of fresh spinach leaves
1 teaspoon olive oil
¼ teaspoon smoked paprika
Salt and black pepper to taste

Instructions:
1. Bring a small pot of water to the boil and cook the sweet potato cubes for 5–7 minutes until just tender. Drain and set aside.
2. Heat the olive oil in a frying pan over medium heat. Add the onion and red pepper, cooking for 4–5 minutes until softened.
3. Stir in the sweet potato and sprinkle with smoked paprika, salt, and black pepper. Cook for another 5 minutes, stirring occasionally, until the edges of the sweet potato are lightly crisp.
4. Add the spinach and cook for 2–3 minutes until wilted. Serve immediately.

Serving Suggestions:
Serve alongside a small salad of mixed greens, orange segments, and a light vinaigrette for a zesty and refreshing balance.

Nutritional Information (Per Serving):
Calories: 180 kcal | Total Fat: 5 g (Saturated Fat: 1 g) | Cholesterol: 0 mg | Fibre: 5 g | Protein: 3 g

Soups, Broths, and Stews

Soups, broths and stews are more than just comfort food—they're a fantastic way to pack your meals with nutrients while keeping them low in cholesterol. These dishes allow you to combine a variety of vegetables, legumes and lean proteins into one hearty bowl, making them perfect for nourishing both your body and soul. They're also an excellent choice for staying hydrated, as many are broth-based and naturally light.

What to Include in Low-Cholesterol Soups, Broths and Stews
- **Vegetables:** Root vegetables like carrots, parsnips and sweet potatoes add natural sweetness and fibre. Leafy greens like spinach and kale provide antioxidants and essential nutrients.
- **Legumes:** Lentils, chickpeas and beans are excellent sources of plant-based protein and fibre to support heart health.
- **Whole Grains:** Add barley, brown rice or quinoa for extra texture and to keep you feeling fuller for longer.
- **Herbs and Spices:** Use fresh or dried herbs like thyme, rosemary or basil, and spices like turmeric or smoked paprika to elevate flavours without relying on salt.
- **Healthy Fats:** Use olive oil sparingly for sautéing vegetables or drizzling on top for a finishing touch.

Tips for Soup and Stew Success
- **Batch Cook:** Prepare large portions and store leftovers in the fridge or freezer for quick, healthy meals throughout the week.
- **Use Low-Sodium Stock:** Opt for low-sodium vegetable or chicken stock to keep your meals heart-healthy and flavourful.
- **Layer Flavours:** Sauté onions, garlic and spices first to create a rich flavour base.
- **Finish Fresh:** Add a handful of fresh herbs or a squeeze of citrus juice just before serving to brighten the flavours.

With these nourishing recipes, you'll enjoy the simple joy of a warm, comforting meal while supporting your low-cholesterol goals. From light and refreshing broths to hearty stews, there's something here for every mood and season!

Sweet Potato and Leek Broth

Preparation Time: 5 minutes | **Cooking Time:** 25 minutes | **Servings:** 2

Ingredients:
1 medium sweet potato (about 200 g), peeled and diced
1 large leek, sliced
2 teaspoons olive oil
500 ml water or low-sodium vegetable stock (available in most supermarkets or health food shops, or homemade to control salt)
1 garlic clove, minced
½ teaspoon fresh thyme leaves (or ¼ teaspoon dried thyme)
Salt and black pepper to taste
Fresh parsley for garnish (optional)

Instructions:
1. Heat the olive oil in a medium pot over medium heat. Add the sliced leek and cook for 3-4 minutes until softened.
2. Add the minced garlic and thyme, and cook for another minute until fragrant.
3. Stir in the diced sweet potato and pour in the vegetable stock (or water). Bring to a boil, then reduce the heat and simmer for 20 minutes, or until the sweet potato is tender.
4. Season with salt and pepper to taste. You can partially blend the broth with a hand blender, leaving some chunks for texture if you prefer.
5. Garnish with fresh parsley and serve warm.

Serving Suggestions:
Serve with a slice of wholegrain bread or a light green salad for a heart-healthy, satisfying meal.

Nutritional Information (Per Serving):
Calories: 150 kcal | Total Fat: 5 g (Saturated Fat: 0.7 g) | Cholesterol: 0 mg | Fibre: 5 g | Protein: 3 g

Mushroom and Barley Broth

Preparation Time: 10 minutes | **Cooking Time:** 30 minutes | **Servings:** 2

Ingredients:
100 g pearl barley
200 g mushrooms, sliced (e.g., chestnut or button mushrooms)
1 medium onion, finely chopped
1 garlic clove, minced
1 tablespoon olive oil
750 ml water or low-sodium vegetable stock (available in most supermarkets or health food shops, or homemade to control salt)
1 teaspoon fresh thyme leaves (or ½ teaspoon dried thyme)
Salt and black pepper to taste
Fresh parsley for garnish (optional)

Instructions:
1. Rinse the pearl barley under cold water and set aside.
2. Heat the olive oil in a medium pot over medium heat. Add the chopped onion and cook for 3-4 minutes until softened.
3. Add the sliced mushrooms and garlic, and cook for another 5-6 minutes until the mushrooms are golden and tender.
4. Stir in the rinsed barley and pour in the vegetable stock (or water). Add the thyme and season with salt and pepper to taste.
5. Bring the mixture to a boil, then reduce the heat and simmer for 25-30 minutes, or until the barley is tender.
6. Garnish with fresh parsley and serve warm.

Serving Suggestions:
Enjoy with a slice of wholegrain bread or a side of steamed greens for an extra boost of fibre and heart-healthy nutrients.

Nutritional Information (Per Serving):
Calories: 250 kcal | Total Fat: 7 g (Saturated Fat: 1 g) | Cholesterol: 0 mg | Fibre: 8 g | Protein: 8 g

Chicken and Vegetable Barley Stew

Preparation Time: 10 minutes | **Cooking Time:** 35 minutes | **Servings:** 2

Ingredients:

1 chicken breast (about 150 g), skinless and diced
75 g pearl barley
1 medium carrot, diced
1 celery stalk, diced
1 medium onion, finely chopped
1 garlic clove, minced
1 tablespoon olive oil
750 ml low-sodium vegetable or chicken stock (available in most supermarkets or health food shops, or homemade to control salt)
1 teaspoon fresh thyme leaves (or ½ teaspoon dried thyme)
Salt and black pepper to taste
Fresh parsley for garnish (optional)

Instructions:

1. Rinse the pearl barley under cold water and set aside.
2. Heat the olive oil in a large pot over medium heat. Add the diced chicken breast and cook for 4-5 minutes until browned on all sides, then remove from the pot and set aside.
3. In the same pot, add the chopped onion, carrot, and celery. Cook for 3-4 minutes until softened.
4. Add the garlic and cook for another minute, then stir in the pearl barley and thyme.
5. Pour in the vegetable or chicken stock, bring the mixture to a boil, then reduce the heat and simmer for 25 minutes.
6. Add the browned chicken back to the pot and simmer for another 10 minutes, or until the chicken is fully cooked and the barley is tender.
7. Season with salt and pepper to taste. Garnish with fresh parsley and serve warm.

Serving Suggestions:

Pair with a slice of wholegrain bread or a side of steamed vegetables for an extra dose of fibre and nutrients.

Nutritional Information (Per Serving):

Calories: 350 kcal | Total Fat: 8 g (Saturated Fat: 1.5 g) | Cholesterol: 40 mg | Fibre: 7 g | Protein: 30 g

Cabbage and White Bean Soup

Preparation Time: 10 minutes | **Cooking Time:** 25 minutes | **Servings:** 2

Ingredients:

150 g white beans (cooked, or use a 400 g tin, drained and rinsed)
200 g green cabbage, shredded
1 medium carrot, diced
1 celery stalk, diced
1 medium onion, finely chopped
1 garlic clove, minced
1 tablespoon olive oil
750 ml water or low-sodium vegetable stock (available in most supermarkets or health food shops, or homemade to control salt)
1 teaspoon dried thyme
Salt and black pepper to taste
Fresh parsley for garnish (optional)

Instructions:

1. Heat the olive oil in a large pot over medium heat. Add the chopped onion, carrot, and celery, and cook for 3-4 minutes until softened.
2. Add the minced garlic and cook for another minute until fragrant.
3. Stir in the shredded cabbage and cook for 2-3 minutes until it begins to soften.
4. Add the white beans and pour in the vegetable stock (or water). Stir in the thyme and season with salt and pepper to taste.
5. Bring the soup to a boil, then reduce the heat and simmer for 15-20 minutes, or until the vegetables are tender.
6. Garnish with fresh parsley and serve warm.

Serving Suggestions:

Enjoy with a slice of wholegrain bread or a small green salad for added fibre and nutrients.

Nutritional Information (Per Serving):

Calories: 220 kcal | Total Fat: 6 g (Saturated Fat: 0.8 g) | Cholesterol: 0 mg | Fibre: 9 g | Protein: 9 g

Lemon and Lentil Soup

Preparation Time: 10 minutes | **Cooking Time:** 25minutes | **Servings:** 2

Ingredients:
100 g red lentils, rinsed
1 medium carrot, diced
1 small onion, finely chopped
1 garlic clove, minced
1 tablespoon olive oil
750 ml low-sodium vegetable stock
or water (available in most
supermarkets or health food shops,
or homemade to control salt)
1 teaspoon ground cumin
1 teaspoon ground coriander
Juice of 1 lemon
Salt and black pepper to taste
Fresh parsley or coriander for
garnish (optional)

Instructions:
1. Heat the olive oil in a large pot over medium heat. Add the onion and carrot, cooking for 3-4 minutes until softened.
2. Add the minced garlic, cumin, and ground coriander, and cook for another minute until fragrant.
3. Stir in the rinsed lentils and pour in the vegetable stock (or water). Bring to a boil, then reduce the heat and simmer for 20 minutes until the lentils are tender.
4. Stir in the lemon juice and season with salt and pepper to taste. Use a hand blender to partially blend the soup, leaving some texture if desired.
5. Garnish with fresh parsley or coriander and serve warm.

Serving Suggestions:
Enjoy with a slice of wholegrain bread or a simple side salad for a light, refreshing, and heart-healthy meal.

Nutritional Information (Per Serving):
Calories: 230 kcal | Total Fat: 7 g (Saturated Fat: 1 g) | Cholesterol: 0 mg | Fibre: 9 g | Protein: 10 g

Salmon and Vegetable Chowder

Preparation Time: 10 minutes | **Cooking Time:** 25 minutes | **Servings:** 2

Ingredients:
150 g skinless salmon fillet, diced
1 medium potato, diced
1 medium carrot, diced
1 celery stalk, diced
1 small leek, sliced
1 garlic clove, minced
1 tablespoon olive oil
500 ml water or low-sodium
vegetable or fish stock (available in
most supermarkets or health food
shops, or homemade to control salt)
100 ml unsweetened almond milk
or semi-skimmed milk
1 teaspoon dried dill (or 1
tablespoon fresh dill)
Salt and black pepper to taste
Fresh parsley for garnish (optional)

Instructions:
1. Heat the olive oil in a large pot over medium heat. Add the leek, carrot, celery, and potato. Cook for 3-4 minutes until the vegetables start to soften.
2. Add the minced garlic and cook for another minute until fragrant.
3. Pour in the vegetable or fish stock and bring to a boil. Reduce the heat and simmer for 15-20 minutes until the vegetables are tender.
4. Stir in the milk and add the diced salmon. Simmer for an additional 5 minutes until the salmon is cooked through.
5. Add the dill and season with salt and pepper to taste. Garnish with fresh parsley if desired and serve warm.

Serving Suggestions:
Serve with a slice of wholegrain bread or a side of steamed green vegetables for a complete, heart-healthy meal.

Nutritional Information (Per Serving):
Calories: 300 kcal | Total Fat: 10 g (Saturated Fat: 1.5 g) | Cholesterol: 30 mg | Fibre: 6 g | Protein: 22 g

Butternut Squash and Coconut Stew

Preparation Time: 10 minutes | **Cooking Time:** 30 minutes | **Servings:** 2

Ingredients:
300 g butternut squash, peeled and diced
1 medium onion, finely chopped
1 garlic clove, minced
1 tablespoon olive oil
200 ml light coconut milk
400 ml water or low-sodium vegetable stock (available in most supermarkets or health food shops, or homemade to control salt)
1 teaspoon ground turmeric
1 teaspoon ground cumin
1 teaspoon fresh ginger, grated (or ½ teaspoon ground ginger)
Salt and black pepper to taste
Fresh coriander for garnish

Instructions:
1. Heat the olive oil in a large pot over medium heat. Add the onion and cook for 3-4 minutes until softened.
2. Add the garlic, turmeric, cumin, and ginger, and cook for another minute until fragrant.
3. Stir in the diced butternut squash and pour in the vegetable stock. Bring to a boil, then reduce the heat and simmer for 20 minutes until the squash is tender.
4. Stir in the coconut milk and simmer for an additional 5 minutes to combine the flavours. Season with salt and pepper to taste.
5. Garnish with fresh coriander and serve warm.

Serving Suggestions:
Serve with brown rice or wholegrain quinoa for a more filling meal.

Nutritional Information (Per Serving):
Calories: 250 kcal | Total Fat: 12 g (Saturated Fat: 7 g) | Cholesterol: 0 mg | Fibre: 6 g | Protein: 3 g

Chicken and Spinach Stew

Preparation Time: 10 minutes | **Cooking Time:** 25 minutes | **Servings:** 2

Ingredients:
1 chicken breast (about 150 g), skinless and diced
100 g fresh spinach, roughly chopped
1 medium onion, finely chopped
1 garlic clove, minced
1 tablespoon olive oil
500 ml low-sodium chicken or vegetable stock (available in most supermarkets or health food shops, or homemade to control salt)
1 medium carrot, diced
1 teaspoon dried thyme
Salt and black pepper to taste
Fresh parsley for garnish (optional)

Instructions:
1. Heat the olive oil in a large pot over medium heat. Add the diced chicken breast and cook for 4-5 minutes until browned, then remove and set aside.
2. In the same pot, add the chopped onion and carrot. Cook for 3-4 minutes until softened, then add the minced garlic and thyme, cooking for another minute.
3. Stir in the chicken stock and bring to a boil. Reduce the heat and simmer for 10-15 minutes until the vegetables are tender.
4. Add the spinach and browned chicken back to the pot. Simmer for another 5 minutes until the chicken is fully cooked and the spinach is wilted.
5. Season with salt and pepper to taste. Garnish with fresh parsley and serve warm.

Serving Suggestions:
Pair with a slice of wholegrain bread or brown rice for a more filling, heart-healthy meal.

Nutritional Information (Per Serving):
Calories: 300 kcal | Total Fat: 10 g (Saturated Fat: 1.5 g) | Cholesterol: 50 mg | Fibre: 5 g | Protein: 28 g

Classic Minestrone with Wholegrain Pasta

Preparation Time: 10 minutes | **Cooking Time:** 30 minutes | **Servings:** 2

Ingredients:
50 g wholegrain pasta (e.g., penne or fusilli)
1 medium carrot, diced
1 celery stalk, diced
1 medium onion, finely chopped
1 garlic clove, minced
1 small courgette, diced
200 g canned chopped tomatoes (no added salt)
400 ml low-sodium vegetable stock (available in most supermarkets or health food shops, or homemade to control salt)
100 g canned kidney beans or cannellini beans (drained and rinsed)
1 teaspoon dried oregano
1 teaspoon dried basil
1 tablespoon olive oil
Salt and black pepper to taste
Fresh basil for garnish (optional)

Instructions:
1. Heat the olive oil in a large pot over medium heat. Add the chopped onion, carrot, and celery, and cook for 3-4 minutes until softened.
2. Add the minced garlic, courgette, oregano, and basil, and cook for another minute until fragrant.
3. Stir in the chopped tomatoes, vegetable stock, and beans. Bring the mixture to a boil, then reduce the heat and simmer for 20 minutes until the vegetables are tender.
4. In a separate small pot, cook the wholegrain pasta according to the package instructions. Drain and set aside.
5. Once the soup is ready, stir in the cooked pasta and season with salt and pepper to taste.
6. Garnish with fresh basil if desired and serve warm.

Serving Suggestions:
Enjoy with a slice of wholegrain bread or a light green salad for a hearty, low-cholesterol meal.

Nutritional Information (Per Serving):
Calories: 250 kcal | Total Fat: 8 g (Saturated Fat: 1 g) | Cholesterol: 0 mg | Fibre: 9 g | Protein: 9 g

Spiced Carrot and Ginger Soup

Preparation Time: 10 minutes | **Cooking Time:** 20 minutes | **Servings:** 2

Ingredients:
300 g carrots, peeled and chopped
1 small onion, chopped
1 garlic clove, minced
1 tablespoon olive oil
1 teaspoon fresh ginger, grated (or ½ teaspoon ground ginger)
½ teaspoon ground cumin
500 ml water or low-sodium vegetable stock (available in most supermarkets or health food shops, or homemade to control salt)
Salt and black pepper to taste
Fresh coriander for garnish (optional)

Instructions:
1. Heat the olive oil in a large pot over medium heat. Add the chopped onion and cook for 3-4 minutes until softened.
2. Add the garlic, ginger, and cumin, and cook for another minute until fragrant.
3. Stir in the chopped carrots and pour in the vegetable stock (or water). Bring to a boil, then reduce the heat and simmer for 15-20 minutes, until the carrots are tender.
4. Use a hand blender to puree the soup until smooth. Season with salt and pepper to taste.
5. Garnish with fresh coriander if desired and serve warm.

Serving Suggestions:
Serve with a slice of wholegrain bread or a side salad for a simple, heart-healthy meal.

Nutritional Information (Per Serving):
Calories: 180 kcal | Total Fat: 7 g (Saturated Fat: 1 g) | Cholesterol: 0 mg | Fibre: 6 g | Protein: 2 g

Spiced Prawn and Vegetable Stew

Preparation Time: 10 minutes | **Cooking Time:** 20 minutes | **Servings:** 2

Ingredients:
200 g prawns, peeled and deveined
1 small onion, chopped
1 garlic clove, minced
1 medium courgette, diced
1 small red pepper, diced
1 tablespoon olive oil
1 teaspoon ground paprika
½ teaspoon ground cumin
400 g canned chopped tomatoes (no added salt)
200 ml water or low-sodium vegetable or fish stock
Salt and black pepper to taste
Fresh coriander or parsley for garnish (optional)

Instructions:
1. Heat the olive oil in a large pot over medium heat. Add the chopped onion and cook for 3-4 minutes until softened.
2. Add the garlic, paprika, and cumin, and cook for another minute until fragrant.
3. Stir in the courgette, red pepper, and chopped tomatoes. Pour in the vegetable or fish stock and bring the mixture to a boil. Reduce the heat and simmer for 10-15 minutes until the vegetables are tender.
4. Add the prawns and cook for an additional 3-4 minutes, or until the prawns are pink and cooked through.
5. Season with salt and pepper to taste. Garnish with fresh coriander or parsley if desired and serve warm.

Serving Suggestions:
Pair with a side of brown rice or wholegrain couscous for a more filling, heart-healthy meal.

Nutritional Information (Per Serving):
Calories: 250 kcal | Total Fat: 9 g (Saturated Fat: 1.5 g) | Cholesterol: 150 mg | Fibre: 5 g | Protein: 22 g

Broccoli and Spinach Detox Soup

Preparation Time: 10 minutes | **Cooking Time:** 15 minutes | **Servings:** 2

Ingredients:
200 g broccoli florets
100 g fresh spinach
1 small onion, chopped
1 garlic clove, minced
1 tablespoon olive oil
500 ml water or low-sodium vegetable stock (available in most supermarkets or health food shops, or homemade to control salt)
Juice of ½ lemon
Salt and black pepper to taste
Fresh parsley for garnish (optional)

Instructions:
1. Heat the olive oil in a large pot over medium heat. Add the chopped onion and cook for 3-4 minutes until softened.
2. Add the minced garlic and cook for another minute until fragrant.
3. Stir in the broccoli florets and pour in the vegetable stock. Bring to a boil, then reduce the heat and simmer for 8-10 minutes until the broccoli is tender.
4. Add the spinach and cook for another 2-3 minutes until wilted.
5. Use a hand blender to puree the soup until smooth. Stir in the lemon juice and season with salt and pepper to taste.
6. Garnish with fresh parsley if desired and serve warm.

Serving Suggestions:
Serve with a slice of wholegrain bread for added fibre, or enjoy as a light, cleansing meal.

Nutritional Information (Per Serving):
Calories: 120 kcal | Total Fat: 7 g (Saturated Fat: 1 g) | Cholesterol: 0 mg | Fibre: 6 g | Protein: 4 g

Herby Mushroom and Sweet Potato Broth

Preparation Time: 10 minutes | **Cooking Time:** 25 minutes | **Servings:** 2

Ingredients:
150 g sweet potato, peeled and diced
150 g mushrooms, sliced (e.g., chestnut or button mushrooms)
1 small onion, chopped
1 garlic clove, minced
1 tablespoon olive oil
600 ml low-sodium vegetable stock or water (available in most supermarkets or health food shops, or homemade to control salt)
1 teaspoon dried thyme (or 1 tablespoon fresh thyme leaves)
Salt and black pepper to taste
Fresh parsley for garnish (optional)

Instructions:
1. Heat the olive oil in a large pot over medium heat. Add the chopped onion and cook for 3-4 minutes until softened.
2. Add the garlic and sliced mushrooms and cook for another 5-6 minutes until the mushrooms are golden.
3. Stir in the diced sweet potato and pour in the vegetable stock. Add the thyme and bring to a boil, then reduce the heat and simmer for 15-20 minutes until the sweet potato is tender.
4. Season with salt and pepper to taste. Garnish with fresh parsley if desired and serve warm.

Serving Suggestions:
Pair this broth with a small side of roasted vegetables or a simple salad made with leafy greens, avocado, and a drizzle of olive oil for added nutrients and heart-healthy fats.

Nutritional Information (Per Serving):
Calories: 180 kcal | Total Fat: 7 g (Saturated Fat: 1 g) | Cholesterol: 0 mg | Fibre: 5 g | Protein: 4 g

Chickpea and Spinach Stew

Preparation Time: 10 minutes | **Cooking Time:** 25 minutes | **Servings:** 2

Ingredients:
1 can (400 g) chickpeas, drained and rinsed
100 g fresh spinach, roughly chopped
1 medium onion, finely chopped
2 garlic cloves, minced
1 tablespoon olive oil
400 g canned chopped tomatoes (no added salt)
500 ml low-sodium vegetable stock or water (available in most supermarkets or health food shops, or homemade to control salt)
1 teaspoon ground cumin
1 teaspoon ground paprika
½ teaspoon ground turmeric
Salt and black pepper to taste

Instructions:
1. Heat the olive oil in a large pot over medium heat. Add the chopped onion and cook for 3-4 minutes until softened.
2. Add the minced garlic, cumin, paprika, and turmeric, and cook for another minute until fragrant.
3. Stir in the canned tomatoes and vegetable stock (or water), and bring the mixture to a boil.
4. Add the chickpeas and reduce the heat to a simmer. Cook for 15-20 minutes, allowing the flavours to blend.
5. Stir in the chopped spinach and cook for another 2-3 minutes, until the spinach is wilted.
6. Season with salt and pepper to taste. Garnish with fresh coriander if desired and serve warm.

Serving Suggestions:
Serve with brown rice, quinoa, or a small side of steamed vegetables for added fibre and heart-healthy nutrients.

Nutritional Information (Per Serving):
Calories: 270 kcal | Total Fat: 10 g (Saturated Fat: 1 g) | Cholesterol: 0 mg | Fibre: 9 g | Protein: 11 g

Tomato and Basil Broth

Preparation Time: 10 minutes | **Cooking Time:** 20 minutes | **Servings:** 2

Ingredients:
1 teaspoon olive oil
1 small onion, finely chopped
2 garlic cloves, minced
400 g tin chopped tomatoes
500 ml vegetable stock (low-sodium)
1 teaspoon dried basil
1 teaspoon dried oregano
1 teaspoon balsamic vinegar
Salt and black pepper to taste
A few fresh basil leaves, torn (for garnish)

Instructions:
1. Heat the olive oil in a saucepan over medium heat. Add the onion and garlic, cooking for 5 minutes until softened.
2. Stir in the chopped tomatoes, vegetable stock, basil, oregano, and balsamic vinegar. Bring to a simmer and cook for 15–20 minutes, stirring occasionally.
3. Season with salt and black pepper to taste.
4. Serve the broth garnished with fresh torn basil leaves.

Serving Suggestions:
Pour the broth over cooked pasta or rice for a more substantial meal.

Nutritional Information (Per Serving):
Calories: 150 kcal | Total Fat: 3 g (Saturated Fat: 0.5 g) | Cholesterol: 0 mg | Fibre: 4 g | Protein: 3 g

Cauliflower and Turmeric Soup

Preparation Time: 10 minutes | **Cooking Time:** 25 minutes | **Servings:** 2

Ingredients:
1 teaspoon olive oil
1 small onion, finely chopped
1 garlic clove, minced
1 teaspoon ground turmeric
1 small cauliflower, chopped into florets
500 ml vegetable stock (low-sodium)
100 ml unsweetened almond milk
½ teaspoon ground cumin
Salt and black pepper to taste
Fresh coriander, chopped (for garnish)

Instructions:
1. Heat the olive oil in a saucepan over medium heat. Add the onion and cook for 5 minutes until softened.
2. Stir in the garlic, turmeric, and cumin, cooking for 1 minute until fragrant.
3. Add the cauliflower florets and vegetable stock. Bring to a boil, then reduce the heat and simmer for 15–20 minutes until the cauliflower is tender.
4. Remove from the heat and blend the soup until smooth using a handheld blender or food processor. Stir in the almond milk and season with salt and black pepper to taste.
5. Return the soup to the heat to warm through if necessary. Serve hot, garnished with fresh coriander.

Serving Suggestions:
Serve with brown rice, quinoa, or a small side of steamed vegetables for added fibre and heart-healthy nutrients.

Nutritional Information (Per Serving):
Calories: 180 kcal | Total Fat: 5 g (Saturated Fat: 0.5 g) | Cholesterol: 0 mg | Fibre: 6 g | Protein: 5 g

Salads and Sides

Why Salads and Sides Are Essential for a Low-Cholesterol Diet
Salads and sides bring balance, variety, and texture to your meals while packing in essential nutrients. Whether you're after the crunch of fresh greens or the warmth of roasted vegetables, these dishes are perfect for complementing mains or enjoying on their own. In a low-cholesterol diet, they serve as a delicious way to incorporate fibre, healthy fats, and plant-based ingredients that support heart health.

What to Include in Low-Cholesterol Salads and Sides
- **Leafy Greens and Vegetables:** Spinach, kale, broccoli, and carrots are rich in vitamins, minerals, and antioxidants that promote heart health.
- **Whole Grains and Legumes**: Brown rice, quinoa, and lentils add bulk and fibre, making salads and sides more satisfying.
- **Healthy Fats:** Olive oil, nuts, and seeds are perfect for light dressings or as toppings to boost flavour and nutrition.
- **Herbs and Citrus:** Fresh parsley, mint, thyme, and a splash of lemon juice can enhance the flavour of any dish without the need for extra salt.

Tips for Delicious Salads and Sides
1. Batch Prep: Roast vegetables, cook grains, and chop herbs in advance to make assembling salads and sides quick and easy.
2. Texture and Colour: Pair crunchy nuts with creamy dressings or roasted vegetables with fresh greens for a balance of textures and a visually appealing plate.
3. Seasonal Eating: Use seasonal produce for maximum flavour and nutrient density.
4. Versatility: Many of these recipes can double as light mains or snacks, perfect for a busy lifestyle.

A Journey of Flavours
In this chapter, you'll find a variety of options to suit every occasion—from light, refreshing salads like the Tomato, Cucumber, and Mint Salad to hearty, warming sides like the Warm Kale and Sweet Potato Mash. These dishes are designed to be simple to prepare, bursting with flavour, and tailored to your low-cholesterol goals.
Let's dive into these wholesome recipes that are as satisfying as they are nourishing!

Spinach and Orange Salad with Walnuts

Preparation Time: 10 minutes | **Servings:** 1

Ingredients:
50g fresh spinach leaves
1 small orange, peeled and
segmented
10g walnuts, roughly chopped
1 teaspoon olive oil
1 teaspoon lemon juice
Pinch of salt and black pepper
Fresh parsley for garnish (optional)

Instructions:
1. In a small bowl, whisk together the olive oil, lemon juice, salt, and pepper to make the dressing.
2. In a serving bowl, combine the spinach leaves and orange segments.
3. Drizzle the dressing over the salad and toss gently to combine.
4. Sprinkle the chopped walnuts on top and garnish with fresh parsley if desired. Serve immediately.

Serving Suggestions:
Pair with a grilled fish fillet, such as salmon or cod, for a balanced low-cholesterol meal.

Nutritional Information (Per Serving):
Calories: 190 kcal | Total Fat: 6 g (Saturated Fat: 1 g) | Cholesterol: 0 mg | Fibre: 6 g | Protein: 3 g

Warm Kale and Sweet Potato Mash

Preparation Time: 10 minutes | **Cooking Time:** 20 minutes | **Servings:** 1

Ingredients:
1 small sweet potato (about 150 g),
peeled and diced
30 g fresh kale, stems removed and
chopped
1 teaspoon olive oil
1 garlic clove, minced
Pinch of salt and black pepper
1 teaspoon lemon juice (optional)

Instructions:
1. Boil the diced sweet potato in a small pot of water for 12-15 minutes until tender. Drain and set aside.
2. While the sweet potato is cooking, heat the olive oil in a pan over medium heat. Add the minced garlic and cook for 1 minute until fragrant.
3. Add the chopped kale to the pan and cook for 3-4 minutes, stirring occasionally, until wilted and tender. Remove from heat.
4. Mash the cooked sweet potato with a fork or potato masher. Stir in the cooked kale, season with salt and pepper, and drizzle with lemon juice if desired.
5. Serve warm.

Serving Suggestions:
Serve alongside grilled chicken breast or turkey slices for a lean, protein-rich meal.

Nutritional Information (Per Serving):
Calories: 180 kcal | Total Fat: 6 g (Saturated Fat: 1 g) | Cholesterol: 0 mg | Fibre: 6 g | Protein: 3 g

Warm Beetroot and Lentil Salad

Preparation Time: 10 minutes | **Cooking Time:** 20 minutes | **Servings:** 1

Ingredients:
1 small beetroot (about 100 g), peeled and diced
50 g cooked lentils (or canned, drained and rinsed)
1 tablespoon olive oil
1 teaspoon balsamic vinegar
1 garlic clove, minced
1 teaspoon fresh parsley, chopped (optional)
Salt and black pepper to taste
1 tablespoon crumbled feta (optional, for garnish)

Instructions:
1. Boil or steam the diced beetroot in a small pot of water for 15-20 minutes, or until tender. Drain and set aside.
2. While the beetroot is cooking, heat 1 teaspoon of olive oil in a pan over medium heat. Add the minced garlic and cook for 1 minute until fragrant.
3. Stir in the cooked lentils and cook for another 2-3 minutes, allowing the flavours to combine.
4. In a bowl, toss the cooked beetroot and lentils with the remaining olive oil, balsamic vinegar, and parsley. Season with salt and black pepper to taste.
5. Garnish with crumbled feta if desired and serve warm.

Serving Suggestions:
Pair with grilled salmon or mackerel for a colourful and nutrient-packed plate. Or stuff into a wholemeal wrap or pitta bread with shredded lettuce for a portable and healthy snack or lunch.

Nutritional Information (Per Serving):
Calories: 230 kcal | Total Fat: 11 g (Saturated Fat: 2 g) | Cholesterol: 5 mg (without feta, 0 mg) | Fibre: 6 g | Protein: 6 g

Sweet Potato Wedges with Spices

Preparation Time: 5 minutes | **Cooking Time:** 25 minutes | **Servings:** 1

Ingredients:
1 small sweet potato (about 150 g), cut into wedges
1 teaspoon olive oil
½ teaspoon ground paprika
½ teaspoon ground cumin
¼ teaspoon ground black pepper
Pinch of salt
2 tablespoons low-fat Greek yoghurt for serving
Fresh parsley for garnish (optional)

Instructions:
1. Preheat the oven to 200°C (180°C fan) or gas mark 6.
2. In a bowl, toss the sweet potato wedges with olive oil, paprika, cumin, black pepper, and a pinch of salt until evenly coated.
3. Spread the wedges on a baking tray in a single layer and bake for 20-25 minutes, turning halfway through, until golden and crispy on the edges.
4. Garnish with fresh parsley if desired and serve with a side of low-fat Greek yoghurt for dipping.

Serving Suggestions:
Add the wedges to a platter with hummus, roasted vegetables, and wholemeal pitta for a Mediterranean-style feast.

Nutritional Information (Per Serving):
Calories: 200 kcal | Total Fat: 6 g (Saturated Fat: 1 g) | Cholesterol: 0 mg | Fibre: 4 g | Protein: 5 g

Roasted Brussels Sprouts with Balsamic Glaze

Preparation Time: 5 minutes | **Cooking Time:** 25 minutes | **Servings:** 1

Ingredients:
150 g Brussels sprouts, trimmed and halved
1 teaspoon olive oil
1 tablespoon balsamic vinegar
½ teaspoon honey or maple syrup (optional)
Salt and black pepper to taste
Fresh parsley for garnish (optional)

Instructions:
1. Preheat the oven to 200°C (180°C fan) or gas mark 6.
2. In a bowl, toss the halved Brussels sprouts with olive oil, salt, and pepper until evenly coated.
3. Spread the Brussels sprouts on a baking tray in a single layer and roast for 20-25 minutes, turning halfway through, until golden brown and crispy on the edges.
4. While the Brussels sprouts are roasting, mix the balsamic vinegar with honey or maple syrup (if using) in a small bowl.
5. Once the Brussels sprouts are done, drizzle them with the balsamic glaze and toss gently to coat.
6. Garnish with fresh parsley if desired and serve warm.

Serving Suggestions:
Add to a bowl of quinoa, brown rice, or bulgur wheat with other roasted vegetables for a hearty and filling meal.

Nutritional Information (Per Serving):
Calories: 140 kcal | Total Fat: 6 g (Saturated Fat: 1 g) | Cholesterol: 0 mg | Fibre: 6 g | Protein: 4 g

Green Bean Salad with Dijon Mustard Vinaigrette

Preparation Time: 10 minutes | **Cooking Time:** 5 minutes | **Servings:** 1

Ingredients:
100 g green beans, trimmed
1 tablespoon olive oil
1 teaspoon Dijon mustard 1 teaspoon lemon juice
½ teaspoon white wine vinegar
Salt and black pepper to taste
Fresh parsley for garnish (optional)

Instructions:
1. Bring a small pot of water to a boil and blanch the green beans for 3-4 minutes, until tender but still crisp. Drain and rinse under cold water to stop the cooking process.
2. In a small bowl, whisk together the olive oil, Dijon mustard, lemon juice, white wine vinegar, salt, and pepper to make the vinaigrette.
3. Toss the blanched green beans with the Dijon mustard vinaigrette until well coated.
4. Garnish with fresh parsley if desired and serve immediately.

Serving Suggestions:
Spoon over a baked potato or sweet potato for a simple, wholesome meal.

Nutritional Information (Per Serving):
Calories: 130 kcal | Total Fat: 10 g (Saturated Fat: 1.5 g) | Cholesterol: 0 mg | Fibre: 3 g | Protein: 2 g

Herbed Brown Rice with Peas

Preparation Time: 5 minutes | **Cooking Time:** 25-30 minutes | **Servings:** 1

Ingredients:
50 g brown rice
50 g frozen peas
1 tablespoon fresh parsley or dill, chopped
1 teaspoon olive oil
1 garlic clove, minced (optional)
Salt and black pepper to taste
1 teaspoon lemon juice (optional)

Instructions:
1. Cook the brown rice according to the package instructions, usually around 25-30 minutes. Once cooked, drain any excess water.
2. In the last 3-4 minutes of cooking the rice, add the frozen peas to the pot to cook through.
3. In a small pan, heat the olive oil over medium heat. Add the minced garlic (if using) and cook for 1-2 minutes until fragrant.
4. Toss the cooked rice and peas with the olive oil and garlic mixture. Stir in the fresh herbs, and season with salt, black pepper, and lemon juice (if using).
5. Serve warm.

Serving Suggestions:
Combine with roasted vegetables, chickpeas, and a dollop of low-fat Greek yoghurt for a filling grain bowl.

Nutritional Information (Per Serving):
Calories: 180 kcal | Total Fat: 5 g (Saturated Fat: 0.7 g) | Cholesterol: 0 mg | Fibre: 4 g | Protein: 5 g

Courgette Ribbons with Lemon and Pine Nuts

Preparation Time: 10 minutes | **Servings:** 1

Ingredients:
1 medium courgette, peeled into ribbons using a vegetable peeler
1 tablespoon pine nuts, lightly toasted
1 teaspoon olive oil
1 teaspoon lemon juice
Zest of ½ lemon
Salt and black pepper to taste
Fresh parsley for garnish (optional)

Instructions:
1. Using a vegetable peeler, peel the courgette into thin ribbons and place them in a bowl.
2. In a small bowl, whisk together the olive oil, lemon juice, lemon zest, salt, and black pepper.
3. Drizzle the dressing over the courgette ribbons and toss gently to coat.
4. Sprinkle the toasted pine nuts on top and garnish with fresh parsley if desired. Serve immediately.

Serving Suggestions:
Arrange on top of toasted wholemeal bread with a dollop of low-fat ricotta or a plant-based cheese alternative for an elegant snack.

Nutritional Information (Per Serving):
Calories: 120 kcal | Total Fat: 9 g (Saturated Fat: 1 g) | Cholesterol: 0 mg | Fibre: 2 g | Protein: 3 g

Cabbage and Carrot Coleslaw with Greek Yoghurt Dressing

Preparation Time: 10 minutes | **Servings:** 1

Ingredients:
50 g white cabbage, finely shredded
1 small carrot, grated
2 tablespoons low-fat Greek
yoghurt
1 teaspoon lemon juice
½ teaspoon Dijon mustard
Salt and black pepper to taste
Fresh parsley for garnish (optional)

Instructions:
1. In a small bowl, whisk together the Greek yoghurt, lemon juice, Dijon mustard, salt, and black pepper to make the dressing.
2. In a larger bowl, combine the shredded cabbage and grated carrot.
3. Pour the dressing over the cabbage and carrot and toss until evenly coated.
4. Garnish with fresh parsley if desired and serve immediately.

Serving Suggestions:
Use as a creamy topping for a baked sweet or regular potato, adding a fresh crunch.

Nutritional Information (Per Serving):
Calories: 80 kcal | Total Fat: 2 g (Saturated Fat: 1 g) | Cholesterol: 0 mg | Fibre: 3 g | Protein: 4 g

Roasted Carrots with Thyme and Olive Oil

Preparation Time: 5 minutes | **Cooking Time:** 25-30 minutes | **Servings:** 1

Ingredients:
2 medium carrots, peeled and cut into sticks
1 teaspoon olive oil
½ teaspoon dried thyme (or 1 teaspoon fresh thyme leaves)
Salt and black pepper to taste
Fresh parsley for garnish (optional)

Instructions:
1. Preheat the oven to 200°C (180°C fan) or gas mark 6.
2. In a bowl, toss the carrot sticks with olive oil, thyme, salt, and pepper until evenly coated.
3. Spread the carrots in a single layer on a baking tray and roast for 25-30 minutes, turning halfway through, until golden and tender.
4. Garnish with fresh parsley if desired and serve warm.

Serving Suggestions:
Serve alongside lean roasted chicken, turkey, or a nut roast for a modern twist on a traditional Sunday lunch.

Nutritional Information (Per Serving):
Calories: 110 kcal | Total Fat: 5 g (Saturated Fat: 0.7 g) | Cholesterol: 0 mg | Fibre: 4 g | Protein: 1 g

Tomato, Cucumber, and Mint Salad

Preparation Time: 10 minutes | **Servings:** 1

Ingredients:
1 medium tomato, diced
½ cucumber, diced
1 tablespoon fresh mint leaves, chopped
1 teaspoon olive oil
1 teaspoon lemon juice
Salt and black pepper to taste

Instructions:
1. In a bowl, combine the diced tomato, cucumber, and chopped mint leaves.
2. In a small bowl, whisk together the olive oil, lemon juice, salt, and black pepper to make the dressing.
3. Pour the dressing over the salad and toss gently to combine.
4. Serve immediately.

Serving Suggestions:
Pair with grilled salmon for a light and main dish.

Nutritional Information (Per Serving):
Calories: 80 kcal | Total Fat: 4 g (Saturated Fat: 0.5 g) | Cholesterol: 0 mg | Fibre: 2 g | Protein: 1 g

Grilled Asparagus with Lemon and Olive Oil

Preparation Time: 5 minutes | **Cooking Time:** 5-7 minutes | **Servings:** 1

Ingredients:
100 g asparagus spears, trimmed
1 teaspoon olive oil
1 teaspoon lemon juice
Salt and black pepper to taste
Fresh lemon zest for garnish
(optional)

Instructions:
1. Preheat a grill or grill pan over medium heat.
2. Toss the asparagus spears with olive oil, salt, and pepper until evenly coated.
3. Place the asparagus on the grill and cook for 5-7 minutes, turning occasionally, until tender and lightly charred.
4. Remove from the grill, drizzle with lemon juice, and garnish with fresh lemon zest if desired. Serve immediately.

Serving Suggestions:
Top the asparagus with a poached egg for a simple yet elegant breakfast or light lunch.

Tip:
To cook a perfect poached egg, bring a small pot of water to a gentle simmer and add a splash of vinegar (optional, to help the egg hold its shape). Crack the egg into a small bowl, then gently slide it into the simmering water. Cook for about 3 minutes until the whites are set but the yolk is still runny. Remove with a slotted spoon and serve immediately.

Nutritional Information (Per Serving):
Calories: 70 kcal | Total Fat: 5 g (Saturated Fat: 0.7 g) | Cholesterol: 0 mg | Fibre: 2 g | Protein: 2 g

Broccoli and Almond Slaw

Preparation Time: 10 minutes | **Servings:** 1

Ingredients:
100 g broccoli, finely chopped
1 small carrot, grated
1 tablespoon sliced almonds, lightly toasted
2 tablespoons low-fat Greek yoghurt
1 teaspoon lemon juice
½ teaspoon Dijon mustard
Salt and black pepper to taste

Instructions:
1. In a small bowl, whisk together the Greek yoghurt, lemon juice, Dijon mustard, salt, and black pepper to make the dressing.
2. In a larger bowl, combine the chopped broccoli, grated carrot, and toasted almonds.
3. Pour the dressing over the broccoli mixture and toss until evenly coated.
4. Serve immediately or chill for a few minutes before serving.

Serving Suggestions:
Include in a traditional-style Ploughman's platter with low-fat cheese or plant-based alternatives, chutney, and wholemeal bread.

Nutritional Information (Per Serving):
Calories: 130 kcal | Total Fat: 6 g (Saturated Fat: 1 g) | Cholesterol: 0 mg | Fibre: 4 g | Protein: 5 g

Roasted Cauliflower with Tahini Dressing

Preparation Time: 10 minutes | **Cooking Time:** 25 minutes | **Servings:** 1

Ingredients:
150 g cauliflower florets
1 teaspoon olive oil
Salt and black pepper to taste
1 tablespoon tahini
1 teaspoon lemon juice
½ teaspoon garlic, minced (optional)
1 teaspoon water (to thin the dressing)
Fresh parsley for garnish (optional)

Instructions:
1. Preheat the oven to 200°C (180°C fan) or gas mark 6.
2. Toss the cauliflower florets with olive oil, salt, and black pepper. Spread them on a baking tray in a single layer.
3. Roast the cauliflower for 20-25 minutes, turning halfway through, until golden and tender.
4. While the cauliflower is roasting, whisk together the tahini, lemon juice, minced garlic (if using), and water in a small bowl to make the dressing. Adjust the consistency by adding more water if needed.
5. Drizzle the tahini dressing over the roasted cauliflower, garnish with fresh parsley if desired, and serve warm.

Serving Suggestions:
Serve with warm lentils or a bean stew for a satisfying and protein-rich vegetarian option.

Nutritional Information (Per Serving):
Calories: 180 kcal | Total Fat: 10 g (Saturated Fat: 1.5 g) | Cholesterol: 0 mg | Fibre: 5 g | Protein: 6 g

Celeriac and Apple Slaw with Lemon-Tahini Dressing

Preparation Time: 15 minutes | **Servings:** 1

Ingredients:
½ small celeriac, peeled and julienned
½ green apple, julienned
½ small carrot, grated
½ tablespoon tahini
Juice of ¼ lemon
½ teaspoon maple syrup
½ teaspoon Dijon mustard
1 tablespoon water (or as needed)
Salt and black pepper to taste
½ tablespoon chopped fresh parsley (for garnish)

Instructions:
1. In a medium bowl, combine the julienned celeriac, apple, and grated carrot.
2. In a small bowl, whisk together the tahini, lemon juice, maple syrup, Dijon mustard, and water until smooth. Adjust the consistency by adding more water if needed. Season with salt and black pepper.
3. Pour the dressing over the celeriac mixture and toss to coat evenly.
4. Garnish with chopped fresh parsley and serve immediately as a side dish or light salad.

Serving Suggestions:
Serve alongside grilled chicken breast, turkey, or tofu for a fresh and tangy contrast.

Nutritional Information (Per Serving):
Calories: 120 kcal | Total Fat: 3 g (Saturated Fat: 0.4 g) | Cholesterol: 0 mg | Fibre: 5 g | Protein: 2 g

Roasted Fennel and Orange Salad

Preparation Time: 10 minutes | **Cooking Time:** 15 minutes | **Servings:** 1

Ingredients:
1 small fennel bulb, sliced thinly
1 orange, segmented
½ teaspoon olive oil
1 handful of watercress
1 teaspoon balsamic vinegar
1 teaspoon fresh dill, chopped
Salt and black pepper to taste

Instructions:
1. Preheat the oven to 200°C (180°C fan). Toss the fennel slices with olive oil, salt, and black pepper, then spread them on a baking tray. Roast for 12–15 minutes, until tender and lightly caramelised.
2. Arrange the roasted fennel and orange segments on a plate with the watercress.
3. Drizzle with balsamic vinegar and sprinkle with fresh dill. Serve immediately.

Serving Suggestions:
Sprinkle a handful of toasted walnuts or almonds on top for an extra layer of texture and flavour.

Nutritional Information (Per Serving):
Calories: 110 kcal | Total Fat: 2 g (Saturated Fat: 0.2 g) | Cholesterol: 0 mg | Fibre: 4 g | Protein: 2 g

Fish and Seafood Mains

Why Include Fish and Seafood in a Low-Cholesterol Diet?

Fish and seafood are excellent sources of lean protein, omega-3 fatty acids, and essential nutrients that promote heart health and help maintain balanced cholesterol levels. Omega-3s, in particular, can reduce inflammation and support overall cardiovascular health. These recipes provide you with creative ways to incorporate fish and seafood into your meals while keeping them flavourful and satisfying.

What Makes These Dishes Perfect for Low Cholesterol?
- **Omega-3-Rich Fish:** Salmon, mackerel, tuna, and sardines are packed with heart-healthy omega-3 fatty acids.
- **Light Cooking Methods:** Grilling, steaming, baking, and roasting help preserve nutrients and avoid added saturated fats.
- **Fresh Herbs and Spices:** Enhance the natural flavours of seafood without relying on heavy sauces or excessive salt.
- **Wholesome Pairings:** These recipes are paired with fibre-rich sides like roasted vegetables, brown rice, or leafy greens for a balanced and nutritious plate.

Tips for Cooking Fish and Seafood
1. Choose Fresh or Frozen: Opt for fresh fish from sustainable sources or high-quality frozen options to maintain nutritional value.
2. Don't Overcook: Fish cooks quickly, so keep an eye on it to retain moisture and texture.
3. Enhance with Citrus: A squeeze of lemon or lime brightens flavours and adds a dose of vitamin C.
4. Prep in Advance: Marinades and herb rubs can be prepared ahead of time to simplify cooking.

A Journey of Flavours

This chapter includes a range of dishes, from light and zesty recipes like Grilled Salmon with Lemon and Dill to comforting casseroles such as Mediterranean Vegetable and Cod Casserole. Whether you're preparing a weeknight dinner or hosting a special meal, these recipes are designed to impress while supporting your cholesterol-lowering goals. Explore these delicious and health-focused recipes to enjoy the best of fish and seafood while nourishing your body and heart.

Grilled Salmon with Lemon and Dill

Preparation Time: 5 minutes | **Cooking Time:** 10-12 minutes | **Servings:** 1

Ingredients:
1 salmon fillet (about 150g)
1 teaspoon olive oil
1 teaspoon fresh dill, chopped (or ½ teaspoon dried dill)
Juice of ½ lemon
Lemon slices for garnish (optional)
Salt and black pepper to taste

Instructions:
1. Preheat the grill to medium-high heat.
2. Rub the salmon fillet with olive oil, and season with salt, black pepper, and fresh dill.
3. Place the salmon fillet skin-side down on the grill. Grill for 10-12 minutes, turning once halfway through, until the salmon is cooked through and flakes easily with a fork.
4. In the final minute of grilling, drizzle the salmon with lemon juice.
5. Serve with extra lemon slices for garnish if desired.

Serving Suggestions:
Serve alongside a crisp salad of mixed greens, cherry tomatoes, cucumber, and a light olive oil and lemon vinaigrette.

Nutritional Information (Per Serving):
Calories: 250 kcal | Total Fat: 14 g (Saturated Fat: 2.5 g) | Cholesterol: 55 mg | Fibre: 0 g | Protein: 27 g

Oven-Baked Sea Bass with Tomatoes and Herbs

Preparation Time: 10 minutes | **Cooking Time:** 15-20 minutes | **Servings:** 1

Ingredients:
1 sea bass fillet (about 150 g)
1 medium tomato, sliced
1 teaspoon olive oil
1 garlic clove, minced
1 teaspoon fresh parsley, chopped (or ½ teaspoon dried parsley)
1 teaspoon fresh thyme leaves (or ½ teaspoon dried thyme)
Salt and black pepper to taste
Lemon wedges for garnish (optional)

Instructions:
1. Preheat the oven to 200°C (180°C fan) or gas mark 6.
2. Place the sea bass fillet on a baking tray lined with parchment paper. Drizzle with olive oil and season with salt, pepper, parsley, and thyme.
3. Spread the sliced tomatoes and minced garlic evenly over the top of the fillet.
4. Bake in the preheated oven for 15-20 minutes, or until the sea bass is cooked through and flakes easily with a fork.
5. Serve with lemon wedges for garnish if desired.

Serving Suggestions:
Complement the dish with wholegrain rice or a quinoa pilaf for a wholesome and satisfying meal.

Nutritional Information (Per Serving):
Calories: 210 kcal | Total Fat: 10 g (Saturated Fat: 1.5 g) | Cholesterol: 45 mg | Fibre: 2 g | Protein: 25 g

Seared Tuna with a Sesame Crust

Preparation Time: 5 minutes | **Cooking Time:** 5 minutes | **Servings:** 1

Ingredients:

1 tuna steak (about 150 g)
1 tablespoon sesame seeds
(white or black, or a mix)
1 teaspoon olive oil
1 teaspoon soy sauce (low
sodium)
½ teaspoon fresh lemon juice
Salt and black pepper to taste
Lemon wedges for garnish
(optional)

Instructions:

1. Pat the tuna steak dry with a paper towel and season lightly with salt and black pepper.
1. In a small bowl, mix the sesame seeds. Press both sides of the tuna steak into the sesame seeds, coating evenly.
2. Heat the olive oil in a pan over medium-high heat. Once the pan is hot, sear the tuna for 1-2 minutes on each side, depending on your preferred doneness (rare to medium-rare is typical).
3. Drizzle the seared tuna with soy sauce and fresh lemon juice.
4. Serve immediately with lemon wedges if desired.

Serving Suggestions:
Serve over a bed of rocket with cherry tomatoes and thinly sliced red onion for a simple yet elegant presentation.

Nutritional Information (Per Serving):
Calories: 220 kcal | Total Fat: 12 g (Saturated Fat: 2 g) | Cholesterol: 55 mg | Fibre: 1 g | Protein: 24 g

Steamed Salmon and Broccoli with Ginger and Soy Sauce

Preparation Time: 5 minutes | **Cooking Time:** 15 minutes | **Servings:** 1

Ingredients:

1 salmon fillet (about 150 g)
100 g broccoli florets
1 teaspoon low-sodium soy sauce
1 teaspoon fresh ginger, grated
1 garlic clove, minced
1 teaspoon sesame seeds (optional, for garnish)
1 teaspoon lemon juice
Salt and black pepper to taste
Fresh coriander for garnish
(optional)

Instructions:

1. In a steamer, place the salmon fillet and broccoli florets. Steam over medium heat for about 10-12 minutes, or until the salmon is cooked through and flakes easily, and the broccoli is tender.
2. While the salmon and broccoli are steaming, mix the soy sauce, grated ginger, minced garlic, lemon juice, salt, and pepper in a small bowl.
3. Once the salmon and broccoli are cooked, drizzle the soy sauce and ginger mixture over them.
4. Garnish with sesame seeds and fresh coriander if desired, and serve warm.

Serving Suggestions:
Serve alongside mashed sweet potatoes seasoned with a pinch of nutmeg for a comforting and nutritious meal.

Nutritional Information (Per Serving):
Calories: 250 kcal | Total Fat: 14 g (Saturated Fat: 2.5 g) | Cholesterol: 55 mg | Fibre: 4 g | Protein: 28 g

Creamy Salmon and Spinach Pasta

Preparation Time: 5 minutes | **Cooking Time:** 15 minutes | **Servings:** 1

Ingredients:
50 g wholegrain pasta
1 small salmon fillet (about 100 g)
50 g fresh spinach
1 teaspoon olive oil
1 garlic clove, minced
2 tablespoons low-fat plain yoghurt
(or a dairy-free alternative)
1 teaspoon lemon juice
Salt and black pepper to taste
Fresh parsley or dill for garnish
(optional)

Instructions:
1. Cook the wholegrain pasta according to the package instructions. Drain and set aside.
2. In a pan over medium heat, add the olive oil and minced garlic. Cook for 1-2 minutes until fragrant.
3. Add the salmon fillet to the pan and cook for 4-5 minutes on each side until cooked through. Once done, use a fork to gently flake the salmon.
4. Add the spinach to the pan and cook for another 1-2 minutes until wilted.
5. Stir in the low-fat yoghurt and lemon juice, mixing well to create a creamy sauce. Season with salt and black pepper to taste.
6. Toss the cooked pasta with the salmon and spinach mixture. Garnish with fresh parsley or dill if desired and serve immediately.

Serving Suggestions:
Pair with a simple side salad of rocket, cherry tomatoes, and cucumber, dressed with lemon juice and a drizzle of olive oil.

Nutritional Information (Per Serving):
Calories: 350 kcal | Total Fat: 14 g (Saturated Fat: 3 g) | Cholesterol: 50 mg | Fibre: 7 g | Protein: 25 g

Grilled Sardines with Garlic and Lemon

Preparation Time: 5 minutes | **Cooking Time:** 8-10 minutes | **Servings:** 1

Ingredients:
2 fresh sardines, cleaned and gutted
1 teaspoon olive oil
1 garlic clove, minced
Juice of ½ lemon
Lemon slices for garnish
Salt and black pepper to taste
Fresh parsley for garnish (optional)

Instructions:
1. Preheat the grill to medium-high heat.
2. In a small bowl, mix the olive oil, minced garlic, lemon juice, salt, and black pepper.
3. Rub the garlic and lemon mixture over the sardines, coating them evenly.
4. Place the sardines on the grill and cook for 4-5 minutes on each side, until the fish is golden and cooked through.
5. Serve with lemon slices and garnish with fresh parsley if desired.

Serving Suggestions:
Pair with a slice of wholegrain or sourdough bread to soak up the lemony juices.

Nutritional Information (Per Serving):
Calories: 220 kcal | Total Fat: 14 g (Saturated Fat: 2 g) | Cholesterol: 80 mg | Fibre: 0 g | Protein: 22 g

Creamy Prawn and Tomato Pasta

Preparation Time: 5 minutes | **Cooking Time:** 15 minutes | **Servings:** 1

Ingredients:
50 g wholegrain pasta
100 g prawns, peeled and deveined
1 small tomato, diced
1 teaspoon olive oil
1 garlic clove, minced
2 tablespoons low-fat plain yoghurt
(or a dairy-free alternative)
1 teaspoon lemon juice
1 teaspoon fresh basil or parsley,
chopped
Salt and black pepper to taste

Instructions:
1. Cook the wholegrain pasta according to the package instructions. Drain and set aside.
2. In a pan over medium heat, add the olive oil and minced garlic. Cook for 1-2 minutes until fragrant.
3. Add the prawns to the pan and cook for 2-3 minutes on each side until they turn pink and are cooked through.
4. Add the diced tomato and cook for another 2-3 minutes until softened.
5. Stir in the low-fat yoghurt and lemon juice, mixing well to create a creamy sauce. Season with salt and black pepper to taste.
6. Toss the cooked pasta with the prawn and tomato mixture. Garnish with fresh basil or parsley if desired and serve immediately.

Serving Suggestions:
Pair with a light green salad featuring mixed leaves, cucumber, and a lemon vinaigrette for a refreshing complement.

Nutritional Information (Per Serving):
Calories: 280 kcal | Total Fat: 10 g (Saturated Fat: 2 g) | Cholesterol: 150 mg | Fibre: 6 g | Protein: 24 g

Mediterranean Vegetable and Cod Casserole

Preparation Time: 10 minutes | **Cooking Time:** 30 minutes | **Servings:** 2

Ingredients:
200 g cod fillets, diced
1 small aubergine (eggplant), diced
1 red sweet pepper, chopped
1 courgette (zucchini), sliced
1 small onion, finely chopped
2 garlic cloves, minced
1 can (400 g) chopped tomatoes (no added salt)
1 teaspoon olive oil
1 teaspoon dried oregano
1 teaspoon dried basil
1 teaspoon paprika
Salt to taste
Fresh basil for garnish (optional)

Instructions:
1. Preheat the oven to 200°C (180°C fan) or gas mark 6.
2. Heat the olive oil in a large pan over medium heat. Add the onion and garlic, cooking for 3-4 minutes until softened.
3. Add the chopped aubergine, red sweet pepper, and courgette to the pan. Cook for 5-6 minutes until the vegetables begin to soften.
4. Stir in the chopped tomatoes, oregano, basil, paprika, and salt. Let the mixture simmer for 5 minutes to combine the flavours.
5. In a casserole dish, spread the vegetable mixture evenly. Layer the diced cod fillets on top.
6. Cover the casserole dish with foil and bake in the preheated oven for 20 minutes. Then remove the foil and bake for another 10 minutes, or until the cod is cooked through and the vegetables are tender.
7. Garnish with fresh basil if desired and serve warm.

Serving Suggestions:
Serve alongside roasted baby potatoes with a sprinkle of rosemary for a Mediterranean-inspired meal.

Nutritional Information (Per Serving):
Calories: 250 kcal | Total Fat: 6 g (Saturated Fat: 1 g) | Cholesterol: 40 mg | Fibre: 6 g | Protein: 28 g

Baked Salmon with Oranges, Lemons, and Herb Blend

Preparation Time: 10 minutes | **Cooking Time:** 15-20 minutes | **Servings:** 1

Ingredients:
1 salmon fillet (about 150 g)
1 orange, thinly sliced
½ lemon, thinly sliced
1 teaspoon olive oil
2 teaspoons fresh dill, chopped
½ teaspoon onion powder
½ teaspoon garlic powder
½ teaspoon paprika
½ teaspoon dried parsley
Salt to taste
Pomegranate seeds for garnish (optional)

Instructions:
1. Preheat the oven to 200°C (180°C fan) or gas mark 6.
2. In a small bowl, mix the fresh dill, onion powder, garlic powder, paprika, dried parsley, olive oil, and salt to create the herb blend.
3. On a baking sheet lined with parchment paper, arrange the orange and lemon slices in a single layer, creating a base for the salmon.
4. Place the salmon fillet on top of the citrus slices.
5. Rub the herb blend over the salmon, coating it evenly.
6. Bake in the preheated oven for 15-20 minutes, or until the salmon is cooked through and flakes easily with a fork.
7. Garnish with fresh pomegranate seeds if desired and serve warm.

Serving Suggestions:
Toss wholegrain pasta with olive oil, lemon zest, and chopped parsley. Serve alongside or under the salmon to soak up the citrus juices and herb flavours

Nutritional Information (Per Serving):
Calories: 260 kcal | Total Fat: 14 g (Saturated Fat: 2.5 g) | Cholesterol: 55 mg | Fibre: 3 g | Protein: 27 g

Lemon and Herb Pasta with Grilled Prawns

Preparation Time: 5 minutes | **Cooking Time:** 15 minutes | **Servings:** 1

Ingredients:
50 g wholegrain pasta
100 g prawns, peeled and deveined
1 teaspoon olive oil
1 garlic clove, minced
Juice and zest of ½ lemon
1 teaspoon fresh parsley, chopped
1 teaspoon fresh basil, chopped
Salt to taste
Fresh parsley or lemon slices for garnish (optional)

Instructions:
1. Cook the wholegrain pasta according to the package instructions. Drain and set aside.
2. In a pan, heat the olive oil over medium heat. Add the minced garlic and sauté for 1-2 minutes until fragrant.
3. Add the prawns to the pan and cook for 2-3 minutes on each side until they turn pink and are fully cooked.
4. Stir in the lemon juice, lemon zest, fresh parsley, and basil. Season with salt to taste.
5. Toss the cooked pasta in the lemon and herb mixture, making sure it's well-coated.
6. Serve immediately, garnished with extra parsley or lemon slices if desired.

Serving Suggestions:
Toss some fresh rocket leaves into the pasta before serving for an extra peppery kick.

Nutritional Information (Per Serving):
Calories: 300 kcal | Total Fat: 10 g (Saturated Fat: 1.5 g) | Cholesterol: 155 mg | Fibre: 6 g | Protein: 24 g

Herb-Crusted Baked Haddock

Preparation Time: 10 minutes | **Cooking Time:** 15-20 minutes | **Servings:** 1

Ingredients:
1 haddock fillet (about 150 g)
1 tablespoon breadcrumbs (wholegrain if possible)
1 teaspoon olive oil
1 teaspoon fresh parsley, chopped (or ½ teaspoon dried parsley)
1 teaspoon fresh dill, chopped (or ½ teaspoon dried dill)
½ teaspoon garlic powder
½ teaspoon paprika
Zest of ½ lemon
Salt to taste
Lemon wedges for serving (optional)

Instructions:
1. Preheat the oven to 200°C (180°C fan) or gas mark 6.
2. In a small bowl, mix together the breadcrumbs, olive oil, parsley, dill, garlic powder, paprika, lemon zest, and salt until well combined.
3. Place the haddock fillet on a baking sheet lined with parchment paper.
4. Press the herb breadcrumb mixture onto the top of the haddock fillet, pressing down gently to ensure it sticks.
5. Bake in the preheated oven for 15-20 minutes, or until the fish is cooked through and the topping is golden and crispy.
6. Serve with lemon wedges if desired.

Serving Suggestions:
Serve alongside steamed broccoli, green beans, or asparagus for a light and nutritious meal.

Nutritional Information (Per Serving):
Calories: 220 kcal | Total Fat: 7 g (Saturated Fat: 1 g) | Cholesterol: 50 mg | Fibre: 2 g | Protein: 28 g

Baked Sea Bass with Lemon and Rocket

Preparation Time: 5 minutes | **Cooking Time:** 12-15 minutes | **Servings:** 1

Ingredients:
1 sea bass fillet (about 150 g)
1 teaspoon olive oil
Juice of ½ lemon
1 handful rocket (arugula)
1 garlic clove, minced (optional)
Salt to taste
Lemon slices for garnish (optional)

Instructions:
1. Preheat the oven to 200°C (180°C fan) or gas mark 6.
2. Rub the sea bass fillet with olive oil and season with salt. Place it on a baking sheet lined with parchment paper.
3. Drizzle the lemon juice over the fillet and sprinkle with minced garlic if using.
4. Bake in the preheated oven for 12-15 minutes, or until the sea bass is cooked through and flakes easily with a fork.
5. Serve the sea bass on a bed of fresh rocket. Garnish with lemon slices if desired.

Serving Suggestions:
Pair with steamed new potatoes tossed in olive oil and fresh parsley.

Nutritional Information (Per Serving):
Calories: 200 kcal | Total Fat: 9 g (Saturated Fat: 1.5 g) | Cholesterol: 45 mg | Fibre: 1 g | Protein: 24 g

Salmon and Vegetable Casserole

Preparation Time: 10 minutes | **Cooking Time:** 25-30 minutes | **Servings:** 2

Ingredients:
200 g salmon fillets, diced
1 small courgette (zucchini), sliced
1 small carrot, thinly sliced
1 small onion, finely chopped
1 garlic clove, minced
1 teaspoon olive oil
100 ml low-sodium vegetable or fish stock
2 tablespoons low-fat plain yoghurt (or a dairy-free alternative)
1 teaspoon fresh dill, chopped (or ½ teaspoon dried dill)1 teaspoon lemon juice
Salt to taste
Fresh parsley for garnish (optional)

Instructions:
1. Preheat the oven to 200°C (180°C fan) or gas mark 6.
2. In a pan, heat the olive oil over medium heat. Add the chopped onion and garlic, cooking for 3-4 minutes until softened.
3. Add the sliced courgette and carrot, and cook for another 3-4 minutes until slightly tender.
4. In a small bowl, mix the low-fat yoghurt, dill, lemon juice, and a pinch of salt.
5. In a casserole dish, layer the sautéed vegetables, followed by the diced salmon fillets. Pour the vegetable or fish stock evenly over the top.
6. Spread the yoghurt mixture over the salmon and vegetables.
7. Cover the dish with foil and bake in the preheated oven for 20 minutes. Then remove the foil and bake for an additional 5-10 minutes, or until the salmon is cooked through and the vegetables are tender.
8. Garnish with fresh parsley and serve warm.

Serving Suggestions:
Serve with a slice of wholegrain or sourdough bread to soak up the creamy casserole juices.

Nutritional Information (Per Serving):
Calories: 300 kcal | Total Fat: 14 g (Saturated Fat: 2.5 g) | Cholesterol: 55 mg | Fibre: 4 g | Protein: 25 g

Baked Haddock with a Light Mustard Glaze

Preparation Time: 5 minutes | **Cooking Time:** 12-15 minutes | **Servings:** 1

Ingredients:
1 haddock fillet (about 150 g)
1 teaspoon olive oil
1 teaspoon Dijon mustard
1 teaspoon lemon juice
½ teaspoon honey (optional for sweetness)
1 garlic clove, minced (optional)
Salt to taste
Fresh parsley for garnish (optional)

Instructions:
1. Preheat the oven to 200°C (180°C fan) or gas mark 6.
2. In a small bowl, mix the Dijon mustard, olive oil, lemon juice, honey (if using), minced garlic (if using), and salt to create the mustard glaze.
3. Place the haddock fillet on a baking sheet lined with parchment paper. Brush the mustard glaze evenly over the top of the fillet.
4. Bake in the preheated oven for 12-15 minutes, or until the haddock is cooked through and flakes easily with a fork.
5. Garnish with fresh parsley if desired and serve warm.

Serving Suggestions:
Accompany with cooked brown rice or quinoa for a wholesome and satisfying meal.

Nutritional Information (Per Serving):
Calories: 200 kcal | Total Fat: 8 g (Saturated Fat: 1.5 g) | Cholesterol: 45 mg | Fibre: 0 g | Protein: 24 g

Mussels with Garlic, Lemon, and Parsley

Preparation Time: 10 minutes | **Cooking Time:** 25-30 minutes | **Servings:** 1

Ingredients:
500 g mussels, cleaned and bearded
1 tbsp olive oil
1 clove garlic, finely chopped
Zest and juice of 1/2 lemon
1 handful fresh parsley, chopped
50 ml dry white wine or vegetable
stock
Salt and pepper, to taste

Instructions:

1. Heat the olive oil in a large pan over medium heat. Add the garlic and cook for 1-2 minutes, until fragrant but not browned.
2. Add the mussels, lemon zest, and white wine (or vegetable stock). Season with salt and pepper, then cover the pan with a lid.
3. Cook for 5-7 minutes, shaking the pan occasionally, until the mussels have opened.
4. Remove from heat and stir in the lemon juice and chopped parsley.
5. Serve immediately, with a slice of wholegrain bread for dipping into the broth.

Serving Suggestions:
Pair with a fresh mixed salad with a light lemon vinaigrette. Add a slice of wholegrain or sourdough bread to soak up the broth.

Nutritional Information (Per Serving):
Calories: 230 kcal | Total Fat: 10 g (Saturated Fat: 1.5 g) | Cholesterol: 0 mg | Fibre: 1 g | Protein: 26 g

Squid with Cherry Tomatoes and Basil

Preparation Time: 15 minutes | **Cooking Time:** 10 minutes | **Servings:** 1

Ingredients:
200 g squid, cleaned and sliced into rings
1 tbsp olive oil
1 clove garlic, finely chopped
100 g cherry tomatoes, halved
1 handful fresh basil, torn
Zest and juice of 1/2 lemon
Salt and pepper, to taste

Instructions:

1. Heat the olive oil in a large frying pan over medium heat. Add the garlic and cook for 1 minute until fragrant.
2. Add the squid rings to the pan and cook for 2-3 minutes, stirring occasionally, until the squid turns opaque.
3. Add the cherry tomatoes and cook for another 2-3 minutes, until they start to soften.
4. Stir in the lemon zest, lemon juice, and fresh basil. Season with salt and pepper to taste.
5. Serve immediately, garnished with extra basil leaves if desired.

Serving Suggestions:
For extra flavour, top with a sprinkle of grated Parmesan.

Nutritional Information (Per Serving):
Calories: 180 kcal | Total Fat: 7 g (Saturated Fat: 1 g) | Cholesterol: 0 mg | Fibre: 3 g | Protein: 22 g

Poultry Mains

The Benefits of Chicken and Turkey in a Low-Cholesterol Diet
Chicken and turkey are excellent protein choices for a heart-healthy lifestyle. These lean meats are naturally low in saturated fats and cholesterol, making them perfect for creating nutritious and satisfying meals. With simple seasonings and fresh herbs, you can transform these versatile proteins into a range of delicious and wholesome dishes.

What Makes These Recipes Ideal?
- **Lean Protein:** Skinless chicken and turkey are naturally low in fat, providing essential protein without the cholesterol burden.
- **Fresh Flavours:** Recipes use fresh herbs, garlic, and citrus to enhance the taste without the need for heavy sauces or excess salt.
- **Versatility:** Whether baked, grilled, or steamed, these recipes adapt to a variety of cooking styles while retaining their nutritious value.
- **Balanced Pairings:** Many recipes are paired with nutrient-rich vegetables, whole grains, or light salads to create well-rounded meals.

Cooking Tips for Poultry
1. **Marinate for Extra Flavour:** Allowing chicken or turkey to marinate enhances the taste while keeping the meat tender.
2. **Don't Overcook:** Lean poultry can dry out quickly, so monitor cooking times to retain moisture.
3. **Season Simply:** Use fresh herbs, spices, and a squeeze of lemon to highlight the natural flavours.
4. **Get Creative:** Poultry works well with global cuisines, from Mediterranean to Asian-inspired dishes.

Highlights from this Chapter
From the Mediterranean-inspired **Chicken Bake with Olives and Tomatoes** to the vibrant **Grilled Chicken Skewers with Herbs**, this chapter offers a variety of low-cholesterol meals to suit every palate. Looking for a creamy indulgence? Try the **Stuffed Chicken Breast with Garlic and Spinach**. Need a quick yet elegant dinner? The **Lemon and Herb Baked Turkey Breast** will not disappoint.

These recipes are perfect for weeknight dinners or entertaining guests while ensuring your meals remain heart-healthy and delicious. Dive into this section and discover just how versatile and flavourful poultry dishes can be!

Mediterranean Chicken Bake with Olives and Tomatoes

Preparation Time: 5 minutes | **Cooking Time:** 25-30 minutes | **Servings:** 1

Ingredients:
1 skinless chicken breast (about 150 g)
½ small red onion, sliced
½ red sweet pepper, chopped
50 g cherry tomatoes, halved
5 black olives, pitted and halved
1 teaspoon olive oil
½ teaspoon dried oregano
½ teaspoon dried basil
½ garlic clove, minced
Juice of ¼ lemon
Salt to taste
Fresh parsley for garnish (optional)

Instructions:
1. Preheat the oven to 200°C (180°C fan) or gas mark 6.
2. In a baking dish, place the chicken breast and surround it with the sliced onion, chopped red pepper, cherry tomatoes, and olives.
3. In a small bowl, mix the olive oil, oregano, basil, minced garlic, lemon juice, and a pinch of salt. Drizzle the mixture over the chicken and vegetables.
4. Bake in the preheated oven for 25-30 minutes, or until the chicken is fully cooked and the vegetables are tender.
5. Garnish with fresh parsley if desired and serve warm.

Serving Suggestions:
Layer the chicken and vegetables on a bed of quinoa, bulgur wheat, or farro, and top with crumbled feta or a sprinkle of toasted pine nuts (optional for extra texture).

Nutritional Information (Per Serving):
Calories: 280 kcal | Total Fat: 12 g (Saturated Fat: 2 g) | Cholesterol: 75 mg | Fibre: 3 g | Protein: 35 g

Lemon and Herb Baked Turkey Breast

Preparation Time: 5 minutes | **Cooking Time:** 20-25 minutes | **Servings:** 1

Ingredients:
1 turkey breast fillet (about 150 g)
½ tablespoon olive oil
Juice of ½ lemon
1 teaspoon fresh thyme (or ½ teaspoon dried thyme)
½ teaspoon fresh rosemary (or ¼ teaspoon dried rosemary)
1 garlic clove, minced
Salt to taste
Lemon slices for garnish (optional)

Instructions:
1. Preheat the oven to 200°C (180°C fan) or gas mark 6.
2. In a small bowl, whisk together the olive oil, lemon juice, thyme, rosemary, minced garlic, and salt.
3. Place the turkey breast fillet in a baking dish and pour the herb and lemon marinade over it, ensuring the turkey is well coated.
4. Bake in the preheated oven for 20-25 minutes, or until the turkey is cooked through and no longer pink in the centre.
5. Garnish with lemon slices if desired and serve warm.

Serving Suggestions:
Serve the turkey over a salad of rocket, spinach, and radishes, topped with pomegranate seeds and a light lemon vinaigrette for a vibrant and zesty option.

Nutritional Information (Per Serving):
Calories: 220 kcal | Total Fat: 9 g (Saturated Fat: 1.5 g) | Cholesterol: 70 mg | Fibre: 0 g | Protein: 30 g

Grilled Chicken with Lemon and Rosemary

Preparation Time: 5 minutes | **Cooking Time:** 15 minutes | **Servings:** 1

Ingredients:
1 skinless chicken breast (about 150 g)
½ tablespoon olive oil
Juice of ½ lemon
1 teaspoon fresh rosemary, chopped (or ½ teaspoon dried rosemary)
½ garlic clove, minced
Salt to taste
Lemon wedges for garnish (optional)

Instructions:
1. In a small bowl, whisk together the olive oil, lemon juice, rosemary, minced garlic, and salt.
2. Place the chicken breast in a shallow dish or resealable bag and pour the marinade over it. Allow the chicken to marinate for 15-30 minutes in the fridge (optional, for enhanced flavour).
3. Preheat the grill to medium-high heat.
4. Remove the chicken from the marinade and grill for 6-8 minutes on each side, or until the chicken is fully cooked and the juices run clear.
5. Serve the grilled chicken with lemon wedges for garnish if desired.

Serving Suggestions:
Pair with a side of roasted root vegetables, such as carrots, sweet potatoes, and parsnips, seasoned with rosemary to echo the flavours of the chicken.

Nutritional Information (Per Serving):
Calories: 250 kcal | Total Fat: 10 g (Saturated Fat: 1.5 g) | Cholesterol: 75 mg | Fibre: 0 g | Protein: 35 g

Stuffed Chicken Breast with Garlic and Spinach

Preparation Time: 5 minutes | **Cooking Time:** 20-25 minutes | **Servings:** 1

Ingredients:
1 skinless chicken breast (about 150 g)
50 g fresh spinach
1 garlic clove, minced
½ tablespoon olive oil
½ teaspoon dried oregano
½ tablespoon low-fat cream cheese (optional)
Salt to taste
Toothpicks for securing

Instructions:
1. Preheat the oven to 200°C (180°C fan) or gas mark 6.
2. In a pan, heat 1 teaspoon of olive oil over medium heat. Add the minced garlic and cook for 1-2 minutes until fragrant. Add the spinach and cook until wilted, about 2-3 minutes. Remove from heat and set aside.
3. If using, mix the cooked spinach with the low-fat cream cheese for a creamier filling.
4. Cut a pocket into the thickest part of the chicken breast, being careful not to cut all the way through.
5. Stuff the spinach mixture into the chicken breast and secure with toothpicks.
6. Rub the outside of the chicken breast with the remaining olive oil, sprinkle with dried oregano, and season with salt.
7. Place the stuffed chicken breast on a baking sheet lined with parchment paper. Bake in the preheated oven for 20-25 minutes, or until the chicken is fully cooked and no longer pink in the centre.
8. Remove the toothpicks before serving.

Serving Suggestions:
Serve alongside a salad of cherry tomatoes, cucumber, red onion, and olives, dressed with lemon juice and olive oil for a refreshing contrast.

Nutritional Information (Per Serving):
Calories: 280 kcal | Total Fat: 12 g (Saturated Fat: 2 g) | Cholesterol: 75 mg | Fibre: 2 g | Protein: 35 g

Honey Mustard Glazed Chicken Breast

Preparation Time: 5 minutes | **Cooking Time:** 20-25 minutes | **Servings:** 1

Ingredients:
1 skinless chicken breast (about 150 g)
½ tablespoon Dijon mustard
½ tablespoon honey
½ teaspoon olive oil
½ garlic clove, minced (optional)
½ teaspoon lemon juice
Salt to taste
Fresh parsley for garnish (optional)

Instructions:
1. Preheat the oven to 200°C (180°C fan) or gas mark 6.
2. In a small bowl, whisk together the Dijon mustard, honey, olive oil, garlic (if using), lemon juice, and a pinch of salt.
3. Place the chicken breast on a baking sheet lined with parchment paper. Brush the honey mustard glaze evenly over both sides of the chicken.
4. Bake in the preheated oven for 20-25 minutes, or until the chicken is fully cooked and golden brown.
5. Garnish with fresh parsley if desired, and serve warm.

Serving Suggestions:
Serve with steamed broccoli, green beans, or tenderstem broccoli for a fresh and vibrant accompaniment.

Nutritional Information (Per Serving):
Calories: 260 kcal | Total Fat: 8 g (Saturated Fat: 1.5 g) | Cholesterol: 75 mg | Fibre: 0 g | Protein: 35 g

Baked Turkey Breast with Paprika and Garlic

Preparation Time: 5 minutes | **Cooking Time:** 20-25 minutes | **Servings:** 1

Ingredients:
1 turkey breast fillet (about 150 g)
½ teaspoon olive oil
½ teaspoon smoked paprika
1 garlic clove, minced
½ teaspoon dried oregano
½ teaspoon lemon juice
Salt to taste
Fresh parsley for garnish (optional)

Instructions:
1. Preheat the oven to 200°C (180°C fan) or gas mark 6.
2. In a small bowl, mix together the olive oil, smoked paprika, minced garlic, oregano, lemon juice, and a pinch of salt.
3. Rub the paprika and garlic mixture over both sides of the turkey breast fillet, coating it evenly.
4. Place the turkey fillet on a baking sheet lined with parchment paper and bake for 20-25 minutes, or until the turkey is cooked through and no longer pink in the centre.
5. Garnish with fresh parsley if desired, and serve warm

Serving Suggestions:
Serve sliced turkey over a bowl of couscous or quinoa mixed with chopped parsley, cherry tomatoes, cucumber, and a drizzle of lemon dressing.

Nutritional Information (Per Serving):
Calories: 220 kcal | Total Fat: 8 g (Saturated Fat: 1.5 g) | Cholesterol: 70 mg | Fibre: 0 g | Protein: 32 g

Steamed Chicken Balls with Spring Onions

Preparation Time: 10 minutes | **Cooking Time:** 15 minutes | **Servings:** 1

Ingredients:

150 g skinless chicken breast, minced
1 garlic clove, minced
1 tablespoon soy sauce (low sodium)
1 teaspoon sesame oil (optional)
1 spring onion, finely chopped
1 tablespoon fresh coriander, chopped (optional)½ teaspoon black pepper
½ teaspoon salt
1 tablespoon breadcrumbs (optional, for binding)

Instructions:

1. In a mixing bowl, combine the minced chicken, minced garlic, soy sauce, sesame oil (if using), chopped spring onion, coriander (if using), black pepper, salt, and breadcrumbs (if using). Mix well until all ingredients are evenly combined.
2. Wet your hands slightly and form the mixture into small balls (about 2.5 cm or 1 inch in diameter).
3. Prepare a steamer or a heatproof plate in a large pot with a lid, adding enough water to steam the chicken balls.
4. Arrange the chicken balls on the steamer rack or the plate, ensuring they are spaced apart to allow steam to circulate.
5. Bring the water to a boil, then reduce the heat to medium. Carefully place the steamer rack or plate in the pot. Cover with a lid and steam for 12-15 minutes, or until the chicken balls are cooked through and firm to the touch.
6. Once cooked, remove from the steamer and serve warm.

Serving Suggestions:

Wrap the chicken balls in crisp lettuce leaves with shredded carrots and a drizzle of hoisin sauce for a fresh and portable option.

Nutritional Information (Per Serving):

Calories: 220 kcal | Total Fat: 8 g (Saturated Fat: 1 g) | Cholesterol: 70 mg | Fibre: 0 g | Protein: 30 g

Chicken and Spinach Curry

Preparation Time: 5 minutes | **Cooking Time:** 25 minutes | **Servings:** 1

Ingredients:

1 skinless chicken breast (about 150 g), diced
50g fresh spinach
½ small onion, finely chopped
1 garlic clove, minced
½ teaspoon fresh ginger, grated
½ tablespoon olive oil
½ teaspoon curry powder
¼ teaspoon ground turmeric
¼ teaspoon ground cumin
100g canned chopped tomatoes (no added salt)
50ml low-sodium vegetable or chicken stock
Salt to taste
Fresh coriander for garnish (optional)

Instructions:

1. Heat the olive oil in a large pan over medium heat. Add the chopped onion and cook for 3-4 minutes until softened.
2. Add the minced garlic and grated ginger and cook for another minute.
3. Stir in the curry powder, turmeric, and cumin, and cook for 1-2 minutes to release the flavours.
4. Add the diced chicken to the pan and cook for 5-6 minutes, stirring occasionally, until the chicken is browned on all sides.
5. Pour in the chopped tomatoes and stock, then bring to a simmer. Reduce the heat and cook for 10-12 minutes, or until the chicken is fully cooked.
6. Stir in the fresh spinach and cook for another 2-3 minutes until wilted.
7. Season with salt to taste and garnish with fresh coriander if desired. Serve warm.

Serving Suggestions:

Serve the curry over a bed of fluffy brown rice to keep the meal hearty and fibre-rich.

Nutritional Information (Per Serving):

Calories: 280 kcal | Total Fat: 10 g (Saturated Fat: 1.5 g) | Cholesterol: 75 mg | Fibre: 4 g | Protein: 35 g

Oven-Baked Chicken with Tomatoes and Basil

Preparation Time: 5 minutes | **Cooking Time:** 20-25 minutes | **Servings:** 1

Ingredients:
1 skinless chicken breast (about 150 g)
1 small tomato, sliced
1 garlic clove, minced1 teaspoon olive oil
1 teaspoon dried basil (or 1 tablespoon fresh basil, chopped)
1 teaspoon balsamic vinegar
Salt to taste
Fresh basil leaves for garnish (optional)

Instructions:
1. Preheat the oven to 200°C (180°C fan) or gas mark 6.
2. Place the chicken breast in a baking dish and drizzle with olive oil. Season with salt and sprinkle the minced garlic and dried basil on top.
3. Arrange the tomato slices over the chicken breast and drizzle with balsamic vinegar.
4. Bake in the preheated oven for 25-30 minutes, or until the chicken is cooked through and no longer pink in the centre.
5. Garnish with fresh basil leaves if desired, and serve warm.

Serving Suggestions:
Place the chicken on a bed of quinoa mixed with cherry tomatoes, parsley, and a drizzle of balsamic glaze for a Mediterranean twist.

Nutritional Information (Per Serving):
Calories: 240 kcal | Total Fat: 10 g (Saturated Fat: 1.5 g) | Cholesterol: 75 mg | Fibre: 2 g | Protein: 35 g

Chicken and Vegetable Bake

Preparation Time: 10 minutes | **Cooking Time:** 20-25 minutes | **Servings:** 1

Ingredients:
1 skinless chicken breast (about 150 g), thinly sliced
1 teaspoon olive oil
1 small carrot, julienned
½ sweet pepper (any colour), sliced
50 g broccoli florets
1 garlic clove, minced
1 teaspoon fresh ginger, grated
1 tablespoon low-sodium soy sauce
1 teaspoon sesame seeds (optional, for garnish)
Salt and black pepper to taste

Instructions:
1. Preheat the oven to 200°C (180°C fan) or gas mark 6.
2. In a bowl, toss the sliced chicken with minced garlic, grated ginger, olive oil, salt, and black pepper.
3. Spread the chicken, carrot, sweet pepper, and broccoli evenly on a lined baking tray.
4. Drizzle the low-sodium soy sauce over the chicken and vegetables.
5. Bake in the preheated oven for 20-25 minutes, or until the chicken is cooked through and the vegetables are tender. Stir halfway through for even cooking.
6. Remove from the oven and serve immediately, garnished with sesame seeds if desired.

Serving Suggestions:
Scoop the chicken and vegetables into crisp lettuce leaves for a fresh and low-carb serving option.

Nutritional Information (Per Serving):
Calories: 280 kcal | Total Fat: 8 g (Saturated Fat: 1.5 g) | Cholesterol: 75 mg | Fibre: 4 g | Protein: 35 g

Steamed Chicken with Ginger and Broccoli

Preparation Time: 10 minutes | **Cooking Time:** 25 minutes | **Servings:** 1

Ingredients:
1 skinless chicken breast (about 150 g)
100 g broccoli florets
1 teaspoon fresh ginger, grated
1 garlic clove, minced
1 teaspoon soy sauce (low-sodium)
1 teaspoon olive oil
Salt to taste
Fresh coriander for garnish (optional)

Instructions:
1. Prepare a steamer or set a heatproof plate in a large pot with a lid, adding enough water to the pot to steam the chicken and broccoli.
2. In a small bowl, mix the grated ginger, minced garlic, soy sauce, olive oil, and a pinch of salt.
3. Place the chicken breast on a heatproof plate and spread the ginger-garlic mixture evenly over the top.
4. Arrange the broccoli florets around the chicken on the plate.
5. Bring the water to a boil, then reduce the heat to medium. Carefully place the plate with the chicken and broccoli in the steamer or pot. Cover with a lid and steam for 12-15 minutes, or until the chicken is fully cooked and no longer pink in the centre.
6. Once done, remove the plate from the steamer, and garnish with fresh coriander if desired. Serve warm.

Serving Suggestions:
Serve the chicken and broccoli over a bed of spinach and rocket, drizzled with a light lemon vinaigrette for a warm, nutrient-rich salad.

Nutritional Information (Per Serving):
Calories: 220 kcal | Total Fat: 6 g (Saturated Fat: 1 g) | Cholesterol: 70 mg | Fibre: 4 g | Protein: 32 g

Turkey Meatballs with Tomato Basil Pasta

Preparation Time: 10 minutes | **Cooking Time:** 25 minutes | **Servings:** 1

Ingredients:
For the Turkey Meatballs:
150 g turkey mince
1 small garlic clove, minced
1 tablespoon fresh parsley, chopped (or 1 teaspoon dried parsley)
1 tablespoon fresh basil, chopped (or 1 teaspoon dried basil)
½ teaspoon onion powder
½ teaspoon salt
½ teaspoon black pepper
1 tablespoon breadcrumbs (optional, for binding)
For the Pasta:
50 g wholegrain pasta
100 g canned chopped tomatoes (no added salt)
½ teaspoon dried oregano
½ teaspoon olive oil
Salt and black pepper to taste
Fresh basil for garnish (optional)

Instructions:
1. In a mixing bowl, combine the turkey mince, garlic, parsley, basil, onion powder, salt, pepper, and breadcrumbs (if using). Mix until well combined.
2. With slightly wet hands, shape the mixture into small meatballs (about 2.5 cm or 1 inch in diameter).
3. Set up a steamer or place a heatproof plate in a large pot with water to steam the meatballs. Arrange the meatballs on the rack or plate, spaced apart for even cooking.
4. Bring the water to a boil, then reduce to medium heat. Place the steamer rack or plate in the pot, cover, and steam for 12-15 minutes, until firm and cooked through.
5. Meanwhile, cook the wholegrain pasta according to package instructions, then drain and set aside.
6. In a saucepan, heat the chopped tomatoes with oregano, olive oil, salt, and pepper over medium heat. Simmer for 5 minutes.
7. Add the steamed meatballs to the tomato sauce and let them simmer for another 2-3 minutes.
8. Serve the turkey meatballs and sauce over the pasta, garnished with fresh basil if desired.

Nutritional Information (Per Serving):
Calories: 350 kcal | Total Fat: 10 g (Saturated Fat: 1.5 g) | Cholesterol: 65 mg | Fibre: 7 g | Protein: 35 g

Spicy Chicken and Sweet Potato Bake

Preparation Time: 10 minutes | **Cooking Time:** 30-35 minutes | **Servings:** 1

Ingredients:
1 skinless chicken breast (about 150 g)
1 medium sweet potato, peeled and cubed
1 teaspoon olive oil
½ teaspoon smoked paprika
½ teaspoon cayenne pepper (adjust to taste)
1 teaspoon dried oregano
1 garlic clove, minced
Salt to taste
Fresh coriander for garnish (optional)

Instructions:
1. Preheat the oven to 200°C (180°C fan) or gas mark 6.
2. In a bowl, toss the cubed sweet potato with olive oil, smoked paprika, cayenne pepper, dried oregano, minced garlic, and salt until well coated.
3. Place the seasoned sweet potatoes in a baking dish. Lay the chicken breasts on top of the sweet potatoes and season with a little more salt and pepper.
4. Bake in the preheated oven for 30-35 minutes, or until the chicken is cooked through and no longer pink in the centre, and the sweet potatoes are tender.
5. Garnish with fresh coriander if desired and serve warm.

Serving Suggestions:
Drizzle with a dollop of low-fat Greek yoghurt mixed with a pinch of cumin and lemon juice for a creamy, cooling element.

Nutritional Information (Per Serving):
Calories: 350 kcal | Total Fat: 9 g (Saturated Fat: 1.5 g) | Cholesterol: 75 mg | Fibre: 5 g | Protein: 35 g

Grilled Chicken Skewers with Herbs

Preparation Time: 10 minutes (plus 30 minutes for marinating) | **Cooking Time:** 10-15 minutes | **Servings:** 1

Ingredients:
1 skinless chicken breast (about 150 g), cut into bite-sized pieces
1 tablespoon olive oil
1 teaspoon fresh parsley, chopped (or ½ teaspoon dried parsley)
1 teaspoon fresh thyme, chopped (or ½ teaspoon dried thyme)
1 garlic clove, minced
Juice of ½ lemon
Salt and black pepper to taste
Skewers (wooden or metal)

Instructions:
1. In a mixing bowl, combine the olive oil, parsley, thyme, minced garlic, lemon juice, salt, and black pepper. Add the chicken pieces and toss to coat. For best results, let marinate in the fridge for 30 minutes (optional).
2. If using wooden skewers, soak them in water for about 15 minutes to prevent burning. Thread the marinated chicken pieces onto the skewers.
3. Preheat the grill to medium-high heat.
4. Place the chicken skewers on the grill and cook for 10-15 minutes, turning occasionally, until the chicken is fully cooked and has nice grill marks. The chicken should be cooked through and no longer pink in the centre.
5. Remove from the grill and serve warm, garnished with extra herbs if desired.

Serving Suggestions:
Serve the skewers with a fresh tabbouleh salad made from bulgur wheat, parsley, mint, tomatoes, and a light lemon dressing.

Nutritional Information (Per Serving):
Calories: 230 kcal | Total Fat: 10 g (Saturated Fat: 1.5 g) | Cholesterol: 70 mg | Fibre: 0 g | Protein: 30 g

Braised Guinea Fowl with Leeks and Mushrooms

Preparation Time: 15 minutes | **Cooking Time:** 40-45 minutes | **Servings:** 1

Ingredients:
1 guinea fowl breast, skinless
1 tbsp olive oil
1 small leek, cleaned and sliced
100 g mushrooms, sliced
1 garlic clove, minced
100 ml chicken stock (low-sodium)
1/2 tsp fresh thyme, chopped
Salt and pepper, to taste

Instructions:
1. Heat the olive oil in a large pan over medium heat. Add the guinea fowl breast and sear for 3–4 minutes on each side, until golden brown. Remove and set aside.
2. In the same pan, add the leek and garlic, cooking for 2–3 minutes until softened.
3. Add the mushrooms and thyme, cooking for another 3–4 minutes, until the mushrooms are tender.
4. Return the guinea fowl to the pan and pour in the chicken stock. Bring to a simmer, cover, and cook for 25–30 minutes, until the guinea fowl is tender and cooked through.
5. Season with salt and pepper, and serve immediately.

Serving Suggestions:
Serve with mashed sweet potatoes or steamed vegetables for a healthy, hearty meal.

Nutritional Information (Per Serving):
Calories: 250 kcal | Total Fat: 9 g (Saturated Fat: 2 g) | Cholesterol: 70 mg | Fibre: 4 g | Protein: 28 g

Stuffed Chicken Thighs with Leek, Spinach, and Mustard

Preparation Time: 20 minutes. | **Cooking Time:** 35-40 minutes | **Servings:** 1

Ingredients:
2 skinless chicken thighs (bone-in or boneless)
1 tbsp olive oil
1 small leek, cleaned and finely chopped
1 garlic clove, minced
100 g fresh spinach, chopped
1 tsp wholegrain mustard
1 tbsp low-sodium chicken stock
Salt and pepper, to taste

Instructions:
1. Preheat the oven to 190°C (170°C fan) or 375°F. Heat olive oil in a frying pan over medium heat. Add the leek and garlic and sauté for 3–4 minutes until softened.
2. Add the spinach to the pan and cook for 2–3 minutes, until wilted. Stir in the wholegrain mustard and chicken stock, and season with salt and pepper. Cook for another 2 minutes until well combined and the mixture thickens slightly. Remove from heat and let it cool slightly.
3. Make a small slit in the side of each chicken thigh to create a pocket. Stuff each thigh with the leek and spinach mixture. Secure with toothpicks or kitchen string.
4. Place the stuffed chicken thighs on a baking tray and season the top with salt and pepper. Roast in the oven for 30–35 minutes, or until the chicken is fully cooked through and golden brown.
5. Let the chicken rest for 5 minutes before serving.

Serving Suggestions:
Serve with steamed new potatoes or roasted parsnips for a hearty side.

Nutritional Information (Per Serving):
Calories: 290 kcal | Total Fat: 12 g (Saturated Fat: 2 g) | Cholesterol: 70 mg | Fibre: 4 g | Protein: 35 g

Beef, Pork, and Lamb Mains

These recipes showcase the best ways to enjoy red meat while prioritising heart health and maintaining a low-cholesterol lifestyle. By choosing lean cuts, incorporating plenty of vegetables, and balancing each dish with nutrient-rich sides, you can still savour the rich, hearty flavours of beef, pork, and lamb without compromising your health goals.

The Benefits of Red Meat in Moderation

Red meat, when enjoyed occasionally, provides essential nutrients such as **iron, zinc, and vitamin B12**, which are vital for energy production, immune health, and red blood cell formation. Including lean cuts of beef, pork, or lamb in your diet now and again can be a delicious way to ensure you're getting these important nutrients, especially when paired with healthy sides to keep your meals balanced.

Managing Cholesterol in Red Meat Recipes

It's true that some of these dishes include red meat, which naturally contains higher levels of cholesterol. However, the recipes have been carefully crafted to use lean cuts and heart-healthy cooking methods, such as grilling, baking, or steaming. Adding fibre-rich sides like whole grains, leafy greens, or pulses helps to reduce cholesterol absorption, making these meals both delicious and nutritious.

How Much Cholesterol is Fine Daily?

For a healthy diet, it's recommended to limit cholesterol intake to **300 mg per day** for most people. For those with high cholesterol or heart disease, the limit is **200 mg per day**. By choosing these recipes and keeping an eye on portion sizes, you can enjoy these hearty dishes while staying within the recommended range. Each recipe's cholesterol content is included to help you make informed decisions.

Tips for Enjoying Red Meat in Moderation

- Opt for lean cuts, such as fillet steak, pork tenderloin, or lamb loin chops.
- Trim any visible fat from the meat before cooking to reduce saturated fat.
- Include plenty of vegetables and whole grains in your meals to balance the richness of red meat.
- Limit red meat to a few times a week and vary your protein sources with poultry, fish, or plant-based alternatives.

By occasionally preparing these red meat dishes, you'll not only enjoy their bold and satisfying flavours but also benefit from their nutritional value. Combined with mindful portion control and fibre-rich accompaniments, these recipes offer a delicious way to add variety to your low-cholesterol lifestyle.

Mediterranean Lamb Meatballs with Tomato Sauce

Preparation Time: 10 minutes | **Cooking Time:** 25-30 minutes | **Servings:** 1

Ingredients:
For the Meatballs:
150 g lean minced lamb
1 garlic clove, minced
1 teaspoon fresh parsley, chopped
(or ½ teaspoon dried parsley)
1 teaspoon fresh oregano, chopped
(or ½ teaspoon dried oregano)
½ teaspoon ground cumin
½ teaspoon salt
¼ teaspoon black pepper
1 tablespoon breadcrumbs (optional, for binding)

For the Tomato Sauce:
200 g canned chopped tomatoes (no added salt)
1 teaspoon olive oil
½ onion, finely chopped
1 teaspoon dried basil
Salt and black pepper to taste
Fresh basil for garnish (optional)

Instructions:
1. In a mixing bowl, combine the minced lamb, minced garlic, parsley, oregano, cumin, salt, black pepper, and breadcrumbs (if using). Mix well until all ingredients are evenly combined.
2. Wet your hands slightly and form the mixture into small meatballs (about 2.5 cm in diameter).
3. Heat the olive oil in a skillet over medium heat. Add the meatballs and cook for about 6-8 minutes, turning occasionally, until browned on all sides. Remove from the skillet and set aside.
4. In the same skillet, add the chopped onion and cook for 3-4 minutes until softened. Stir in the canned chopped tomatoes, dried basil, salt, and black pepper. Bring to a simmer and cook for about 5 minutes.
5. Add the browned meatballs back to the skillet with the tomato sauce. Simmer for an additional 10-15 minutes, until the meatballs are cooked through, and the sauce has thickened.
6. Garnish with fresh basil if desired and serve warm.

Serving Suggestions:
Place the meatballs over fluffy couscous mixed with chopped parsley, cucumber, and a squeeze of lemon for a vibrant, refreshing dish.

Nutritional Information (Per Serving):
Calories: 360 kcal | Total Fat: 12 g (Saturated Fat: 4 g) | Cholesterol: 70 mg | Fibre: 4 g | Protein: 30 g

Beef and Vegetable Chilli (with Beans)

Preparation Time: 10 minutes | **Cooking Time:** 30 minutes | **Servings:** 1

Ingredients:
100 g lean minced beef
½ small onion, finely chopped
1 garlic clove, minced
½ red sweet pepper, chopped
½ carrot, diced
100 g canned chopped tomatoes (no added salt)
50 g canned kidney beans, drained and rinsed
1 teaspoon olive oil
1 teaspoon chilli powder (adjust to taste)
½ teaspoon ground cumin
½ teaspoon dried oregano
Salt and black pepper to taste
Fresh coriander for garnish (optional)

Instructions:
1. Heat the olive oil in a saucepan over medium heat. Add the chopped onion and garlic, cooking for 3-4 minutes until softened.
2. Add the minced beef to the pan and cook for 5-6 minutes, stirring occasionally, until browned.
3. Stir in the chopped red sweet pepper and carrot, cooking for another 3-4 minutes until the vegetables begin to soften.
4. Add the canned chopped tomatoes, kidney beans, chilli powder, cumin, oregano, salt, and black pepper. Bring the mixture to a simmer.
5. Reduce the heat and let the chilli cook for about 20 minutes, stirring occasionally, until the vegetables are tender, and the flavours have melded together.
6. Serve warm, garnished with fresh coriander if desired.

Serving Suggestions:
Thin out the chilli with additional stock to turn it into a spicy soup, served with a wholemeal roll.

Nutritional Information (Per Serving):
Calories: 350 kcal | Total Fat: 10 g (Saturated Fat: 3 g) | Cholesterol: 70 mg | Fibre: 8 g | Protein: 30 g

Steamed Beef and Vegetable Dumplings

Preparation Time: 15 minutes | **Cooking Time:** 15-20 minutes | **Servings:** 1

Ingredients:

For the Dumpling Filling:
100g lean minced beef
1 small garlic clove, minced
1 tablespoon fresh coriander, chopped (or ½ teaspoon dried coriander)
½ small carrot, finely grated
1 spring onion, finely chopped
½ teaspoon soy sauce (low-sodium)
½ teaspoon black pepper
Salt to taste

For the Dumpling Wrappers:
50g plain wholemeal flour
30ml water
A pinch of salt

Instructions:

1. In a bowl, combine the wholemeal flour and a pinch of salt. Gradually add the water, mixing until a dough forms. Knead for a couple of minutes until smooth, then cover with a damp cloth and set aside.
2. In a separate bowl, combine the minced beef, minced garlic, coriander, grated carrot, chopped spring onion, soy sauce, black pepper, and salt. Mix well until fully combined.
3. Divide the dough into small pieces (about the size of a golf ball). Roll each piece into a circle, approximately 5 cm (about 2 inches) in diameter. Place a spoonful of the beef filling in the centre of each wrapper. Fold the dough over the filling and pinch the edges to seal, ensuring no filling escapes.
4. Set up a steamer or place a heatproof plate inside a pot with a lid. Add enough water to steam the dumplings, making sure the water doesn't touch the dumplings.
5. Arrange the dumplings in the steamer basket or on the plate, ensuring they are spaced apart. Cover and steam for 15-20 minutes, or until the beef is fully cooked and the dumplings are firm.
6. Remove the dumplings from the steamer.

Serving Suggestions:
Serve warm, optionally garnished with extra coriander.

Nutritional Information (Per Serving):
Calories: 320 kcal | Total Fat: 8 g (Saturated Fat: 2 g) | Cholesterol: 60 mg | Fibre: 5 g | Protein: 25 g

Grilled Lamb Chops with Mint Yoghurt Sauce

Preparation Time: 10 minutes (plus 30 minutes for marinating) | **Cooking Time:** 10-12 minutes | **Servings:** 1

Ingredients:
2 lean lamb chops (about 150 g total)
1 teaspoon olive oil
½ teaspoon dried oregano
½ teaspoon garlic powder
Salt and black pepper to taste

For the Mint Yoghurt Sauce:
2 tablespoons low-fat natural yoghurt
1 tablespoon fresh mint, chopped (or 1 teaspoon dried mint)
½ teaspoon lemon juice
Salt to taste

Instructions:

1. In a small bowl, mix the olive oil, oregano, garlic powder, salt, and black pepper. Rub the mixture onto the lamb chops and let them marinate in the fridge for 30 minutes for enhanced flavour (optional).
2. In a separate bowl, combine the low-fat natural yoghurt, chopped mint, lemon juice, and a pinch of salt. Mix well and set aside.
3. Preheat the grill to medium-high heat. Place the marinated lamb chops on the grill and cook for 5-6 minutes on each side, or until they reach your desired level of doneness.
4. Remove the lamb chops from the grill and let them rest for a couple of minutes. Serve warm with the mint yoghurt sauce on the side.

Serving Suggestions:
Serve the lamb chops alongside roasted new potatoes seasoned with rosemary and garlic for a classic pairing.

Nutritional Information (Per Serving):
Calories: 280 kcal | Total Fat: 10 g (Saturated Fat: 1.5 g) | Cholesterol: 75 mg | Fibre: 4 g | Protein: 35 g

Baked Flank Steak with Garlic and Rosemary

Preparation Time: 10 minutes | **Cooking Time:** 20-25 minutes | **Servings:** 1

Ingredients:
150 g lean flank steak
1 tablespoon olive oil
2 garlic cloves, minced
1 teaspoon fresh rosemary, chopped
(or ½ teaspoon dried rosemary)
Juice of ½ lemon
Salt and black pepper to taste

Instructions:
1. Preheat the oven to 200°C (180°C fan) or gas mark 6.
2. In a small bowl, mix the olive oil, minced garlic, rosemary, lemon juice, salt, and black pepper.
3. Place the flank steak in a shallow dish and pour the marinade over it, ensuring the steak is well coated. Let it marinate for about 15-30 minutes if time allows.
4. Place the marinated flank steak on a baking sheet lined with parchment paper. Bake in the preheated oven for 20-25 minutes, or until the steak reaches your desired level of doneness (medium-rare is approximately 57°C/135°F).
5. Remove the steak from the oven and let it rest for about 5 minutes before slicing against the grain.
6. Serve warm, optionally garnished with extra rosemary or lemon slices.

Serving Suggestions:
Pair with a wholegrain rice pilaf flavoured with garlic, parsley, and a handful of toasted almonds for a hearty side.

Nutritional Information (Per Serving):
Calories: 280 kcal | Total Fat: 12 g (Saturated Fat: 4 g) | Cholesterol: 75 mg | Fibre: 0 g | Protein: 36 g

Brown Rice with Spiced Pork and Vegetables

Preparation Time: 5 minutes | **Cooking Time:** 20 minutes | **Servings:** 1

Ingredients:
75 g brown rice 100 g lean pork mince
½ small onion, finely chopped
½ carrot, diced
½ sweet pepper, chopped
1 garlic clove, minced
1 teaspoon olive oil
½ teaspoon paprika
½ teaspoon dried thyme
Salt and black pepper to taste

Instructions:
1. Cook the brown rice according to the package instructions. Set aside when done.
2. In a saucepan, heat the olive oil over medium heat. Add the chopped onion and cook for 2-3 minutes until softened.
3. Add the lean pork mince to the pan and cook for 5-6 minutes, stirring occasionally, until browned.
4. Stir in the diced carrot, chopped sweet pepper, minced garlic, paprika, thyme, salt, and black pepper. Cook for another 4-5 minutes, until the vegetables are tender.
5. Add the cooked brown rice to the pork and vegetable mixture. Stir well to combine and heat through.
6. Serve warm.

Serving Suggestions:
Serve the pork and rice over steamed broccoli, kale, or spinach for added nutrients and colour.

Nutritional Information (Per Serving):
Calories: 400 kcal | Total Fat: 10 g (Saturated Fat: 3 g) | Cholesterol: 70 mg | Fibre: 6 g | Protein: 30 g

Stuffed Peppers with Lean Beef and Quinoa

Preparation Time: 10 minutes | **Cooking Time:** 20 minutes | **Servings:** 1

Ingredients:
1 large pepper (any colour)
100 g lean minced beef
50 g cooked quinoa
½ small onion, finely chopped
1 garlic clove, minced
100 g canned chopped tomatoes (no added salt)
1 teaspoon olive oi
1½ teaspoon dried oregano
Salt and black pepper to taste
Fresh parsley for garnish (optional)

Instructions:
1. Preheat the oven to 200°C (180°C fan) or gas mark 6.
2. Cut the top off the sweet pepper and remove the seeds and membranes. Set aside.
3. In a skillet, heat the olive oil over medium heat. Add the chopped onion and minced garlic, cooking for 3-4 minutes until softened.
4. Add the minced beef to the skillet and cook for 5-6 minutes, stirring occasionally, until browned.
5. Stir in the cooked quinoa, canned chopped tomatoes, oregano, salt, and black pepper. Cook for another 2-3 minutes, until heated through.
6. Stuff the pepper with the beef and quinoa mixture, packing it down gently.
7. Place the stuffed pepper in a baking dish and cover with foil. Bake in the preheated oven for 25-30 minutes, or until the pepper is tender.
8. Remove the foil and bake for an additional 5 minutes if you prefer a slightly charred top.
9. Garnish with fresh parsley if desired and serve warm.

Serving Suggestions:
Sprinkle with a dairy-free cheese substitute or a small amount of grated low-fat cheese before baking for a melty topping.

Nutritional Information (Per Serving):
Calories: 320 kcal | Total Fat: 10 g (Saturated Fat: 3 g) | Cholesterol: 70 mg | Fibre: 5 g | Protein: 30 g

Baked Beef and Vegetable Casserole

Preparation Time: 10 minutes | **Cooking Time:** 30-35 minutes | **Servings:** 1

Ingredients:
100 g lean minced beef
½ small onion, finely chopped
½ colour pepper, chopped
100 g broccoli florets
1 garlic clove, minced
100 g canned chopped tomatoes (no added salt)
1 teaspoon olive oil
½ teaspoon dried oregano
Salt and black pepper to taste

Instructions:
1. Preheat the oven to 200°C (180°C fan) or gas mark 6.
2. In a baking dish, combine the minced beef, chopped onion, sweet pepper, broccoli florets, minced garlic, canned tomatoes, olive oil, oregano, salt, and black pepper. Mix well until all ingredients are evenly distributed.
3. Cover the dish with foil and bake in the preheated oven for 25-30 minutes, or until the beef is cooked through and the vegetables are tender.
4. Remove the foil and bake for an additional 5 minutes to allow any excess liquid to evaporate.
5. Serve warm.

Serving Suggestions:
Garnish with freshly chopped parsley, coriander, or basil for added colour and flavour.

Nutritional Information (Per Serving):
Calories: 280 kcal | Total Fat: 10 g (Saturated Fat: 3 g) | Cholesterol: 65 mg | Fibre: 4 g | Protein: 30 g

Wholegrain Pasta with Beef and Tomato Sauce

Preparation Time: 5 minutes | **Cooking Time:** 15 minutes | **Servings:** 1

Ingredients:
50 g wholegrain pasta
100 g lean minced beef
100 g canned chopped tomatoes (no added salt)
½ small onion, finely chopped
1 garlic clove, minced
1 teaspoon olive oil
½ teaspoon dried oregano
Salt and black pepper to taste
Fresh basil for garnish (optional)

Instructions:
1. Cook the wholegrain pasta according to the package instructions. Drain and set aside.
2. In a saucepan, heat the olive oil over medium heat. Add the chopped onion and cook for 2-3 minutes until softened.
3. Add the minced beef to the pan and cook for 5-6 minutes, stirring occasionally, until browned.
4. Stir in the minced garlic, canned chopped tomatoes, oregano, salt, and black pepper. Bring to a simmer and cook for another 5 minutes until the sauce is heated through.
5. Combine the cooked pasta with the beef and tomato sauce, mixing well to coat.
6. Serve warm, garnished with fresh basil if desired

Serving Suggestions:
Pair with a light salad of rocket, cucumber, and cherry tomatoes, dressed with a lemon vinaigrette for freshness.

Nutritional Information (Per Serving):
Calories: 350 kcal | Total Fat: 10 g (Saturated Fat: 3 g) | Cholesterol: 70 mg | Fibre: 7 g | Protein: 30 g

Lamb and Vegetable Stew

Preparation Time: 10 minutes | **Cooking Time:** 30-35 minutes | **Servings:** 1

Ingredients:
100 g lean lamb, diced (such as leg or shoulder)
1 teaspoon olive oil
½ small onion, chopped
1 garlic clove, minced
1 small carrot, diced
½ potato, diced
100 g canned chopped tomatoes (no added salt)
150 ml low-sodium vegetable or chicken stock
½ teaspoon dried thyme
Salt and black pepper to taste

Instructions:
1. In a saucepan, heat the olive oil over medium heat. Add the chopped onion and garlic, cooking for 2-3 minutes until softened.
2. Add the diced lamb to the pan and brown for about 5 minutes.
3. Stir in the diced carrot and potato, cooking for another 2-3 minutes.
4. Add the canned chopped tomatoes, stock, dried thyme, salt, and black pepper. Bring to a simmer.
5. Reduce the heat and cover the saucepan. Let the stew cook for 20-25 minutes, or until the lamb is tender and the vegetables are cooked through.
6. Serve warm, optionally garnished with fresh herbs.

Serving Suggestions:
Serve with a slice of warm wholegrain or sourdough bread to soak up the hearty stew juices.

Nutritional Information (Per Serving):
Calories: 320 kcal | Total Fat: 10 g (Saturated Fat: 4 g) | Cholesterol: 70 mg | Fibre: 4 g | Protein: 30 g

Brown Rice with Lean Beef and Vegetables

Preparation Time: 5 minutes | **Cooking Time:** 20 minutes | **Servings:** 1

Ingredients:
75 g brown rice
100 g lean minced beef
½ small onion, finely chopped
½ colour pepper, chopped
50 g broccoli florets1 garlic clove, minced
1 teaspoon olive oil
½ teaspoon soy sauce (low sodium)
Salt and black pepper to taste

Instructions:
1. Cook the brown rice according to the package instructions. Set aside when done.
2. In a saucepan, heat the olive oil over medium heat. Add the chopped onion and cook for 2-3 minutes until softened.
3. Add the lean minced beef to the pan and cook for 5-6 minutes, stirring occasionally, until browned.
4. Stir in the chopped sweet pepper, broccoli florets, and minced garlic. Cook for another 4-5 minutes, until the vegetables are tender.
5. Add the cooked brown rice and soy sauce to the beef and vegetable mixture. Stir well to combine and heat through.
6. Season with salt and black pepper to taste and serve warm.

Serving Suggestions:
Serve with a dollop of low-fat Greek yoghurt mixed with lemon juice and a pinch of cumin for a tangy topping.

Nutritional Information (Per Serving):
Calories: 400 kcal | Total Fat: 10 g (Saturated Fat: 3 g) | Cholesterol: 70 mg | Fibre: 6 g | Protein: 30 g

Baked Pork Fillet with Herbs

Preparation Time: 10 minutes | **Cooking Time:** 25-30 minutes | **Servings:** 1

Ingredients:
150g pork fillet
1 teaspoon olive oil
1 teaspoon fresh rosemary, chopped (or ½ teaspoon dried rosemary)
1 teaspoon fresh thyme, chopped (or ½ teaspoon dried thyme)
1 garlic clove, minced
Juice of ½ lemon
Salt and black pepper to taste

Instructions:
1. Preheat the oven to 200°C (180°C fan) or gas mark 6.
2. In a small bowl, mix the olive oil, rosemary, thyme, minced garlic, lemon juice, salt, and black pepper.
3. Rub the herb mixture all over the pork fillet, ensuring it is well coated.
4. Place the seasoned pork fillet on a baking sheet lined with parchment paper.
5. Bake in the preheated oven for 25-30 minutes, or until the pork is cooked through and the internal temperature reaches 65°C (145°F).
6. Remove from the oven and let the pork rest for about 5 minutes before slicing.
7. Serve warm, optionally garnished with extra herbs.

Serving Suggestions:
Pair with roasted Brussels sprouts tossed in balsamic glaze for a tangy and flavourful side.

Nutritional Information (Per Serving):
Calories: 250 kcal | Total Fat: 10 g (Saturated Fat: 3 g) | Cholesterol: 75 mg | Fibre: 0 g | Protein: 35 g

Herb-Crusted Lamb Cutlets

Preparation Time: 10 minutes | **Cooking Time:** 15 minutes | **Servings:** 1

Ingredients:
2 lean lamb cutlets (about 150 g total)
1 teaspoon olive oil
1 teaspoon fresh parsley, chopped (or ½ teaspoon dried parsley)
1 teaspoon fresh mint, chopped (or ½ teaspoon dried mint)
1 garlic clove, minced
Salt and black pepper to taste

Instructions:
1. Preheat the oven to 200°C (180°C fan) or gas mark 6.
2. In a small bowl, mix the olive oil, parsley, mint, minced garlic, salt, and black pepper to form a paste.
3. Rub the herb mixture over both sides of the lamb cutlets, ensuring they are well coated.
4. Place the lamb cutlets on a baking sheet lined with parchment paper.
5. Bake in the preheated oven for 12-15 minutes, or until the lamb is cooked to your desired level of doneness (medium is about 60°C/140°F).
6. Remove from the oven and let rest for a few minutes before serving.

Serving Suggestions:
Pair with slices of grilled aubergine drizzled with olive oil and a sprinkle of oregano for a Mediterranean-inspired plate.

Nutritional Information (Per Serving):
Calories: 280 kcal | Total Fat: 15 g (Saturated Fat: 6 g) | Cholesterol: 75 mg | Fibre: 0 g | Protein: 28 g

Herb-Crusted Fillet Steak with Mustard Sauce

Preparation Time: 10 minutes | **Cooking Time:** 25-30 minutes | **Servings:** 1

Ingredients:
150 g lean fillet steak
1 teaspoon olive oil
1 teaspoon fresh thyme, chopped (or ½ teaspoon dried thyme)
1 teaspoon fresh rosemary, chopped (or ½ teaspoon dried rosemary)1 garlic clove, minced
Salt and black pepper to taste
1 tablespoon wholegrain mustard
1 teaspoon low-fat natural yoghurt
½ teaspoon lemon juice
Salt and black pepper to taste

Instructions:
1. Preheat the oven to 200°C (180°C fan) or gas mark 6.
2. In a small bowl, mix the olive oil, thyme, rosemary, minced garlic, salt, and black pepper to create a paste.
3. Rub the herb mixture all over the fillet steak, ensuring it is well coated.
4. Place the fillet steak on a baking sheet lined with parchment paper and bake in the preheated oven for 25-30 minutes, or until it reaches your desired level of doneness (medium is about 60°C/140°F).
5. While the steak is baking, prepare the mustard sauce by mixing the wholegrain mustard, low-fat yoghurt, lemon juice, salt, and black pepper in a small bowl until well combined.
6. Once the steak is cooked, remove it from the oven and let it rest for a few minutes before slicing.
7. Serve the sliced fillet steak warm, drizzled with the mustard sauce.

Serving Suggestions:
Replace traditional mash with creamy cauliflower mash for a low-carb alternative that pairs beautifully with the mustard sauce.

Nutritional Information (Per Serving):
Calories: 320 kcal | Total Fat: 12 g (Saturated Fat: 4 g) | Cholesterol: 70 mg | Fibre: 0 g | Protein: 40 g

Lamb Koftas with Minted Yoghurt and Quinoa Salad

Preparation Time: 20 minutes | **Cooking Time:** 15-20 minutes | **Servings:** 1

Ingredients:
100 g lean lamb mince
1 tbsp fresh parsley, finely chopped
1 tbsp fresh mint, finely chopped
1 small garlic clove, minced
1 tsp ground cumin
1/2 tsp ground coriander
1/2 tsp ground cinnamon
Salt and pepper, to taste
1 tsp olive oil (for cooking)
1/2 cup quinoa, cooked
1 tbsp fresh mint, chopped (for the salad)
1 tbsp lemon juice
2 tbsp low-fat natural yoghurt
1/2 tsp dried mint (for the yoghurt)

Instructions:

1. In a bowl, combine the lamb mince with the parsley, fresh mint, garlic, cumin, coriander, cinnamon, salt, and pepper. Mix well and form into small, sausage-shaped koftas.
2. Heat the olive oil in a frying pan over medium heat. Add the koftas and cook for 10–12 minutes, turning occasionally, until fully cooked and browned on all sides.
3. While the koftas are cooking, prepare the quinoa salad. In a small bowl, combine the cooked quinoa with the fresh mint and lemon juice. Season with salt and pepper to taste.
4. In another small bowl, mix the yoghurt with the dried mint and a pinch of salt to make a refreshing minted yoghurt sauce.
5. Serve the lamb koftas with the quinoa salad and a dollop of minted yoghurt.

Serving Suggestions:
Serve with a simple cucumber and tomato salad to balance the richness of the lamb koftas.

Nutritional Information (Per Serving):
Calories: 320 kcal | Total Fat: 12 g (Saturated Fat: 3 g) | Cholesterol: 70 mg | Fibre: 6 g | Protein: 30 g

Beef and Mushroom Stroganoff with Cauliflower Rice

Preparation Time: 20 minutes | **Cooking Time:** 25-30 minutes | **Servings:** 1

Ingredients:
150 g lean beef fillet, thinly sliced
1 tbsp olive oil
1 small onion, finely chopped
1 garlic clove, minced
100 g mushrooms, sliced
1 tsp smoked paprika
100 ml low-sodium beef stock
2 tbsp low-fat sour cream or natural yoghurt
1 tbsp Dijon mustard
Salt and pepper, to taste
1/2 head of cauliflower, grated or riced
Fresh parsley, chopped, for garnish

Instructions:

1. Heat the olive oil in a large frying pan over medium-high heat. Add the beef fillet and sear for 2-3 minutes on each side, until browned but not fully cooked through. Remove the beef from the pan and set aside.
2. In the same pan, add the onion and garlic and cook for 2–3 minutes until softened. Add the sliced mushrooms and smoked paprika and cook for another 5 minutes until the mushrooms release their juices and become tender.
3. Pour in the beef stock and stir in the Dijon mustard. Let it simmer for 5–7 minutes until the sauce reduces slightly.
4. Return the beef to the pan and stir in the low-fat sour cream (or yoghurt). Cook for an additional 2–3 minutes, until the beef is fully cooked and the sauce is creamy. Season with salt and pepper to taste.
5. Meanwhile, heat a separate pan over medium heat and lightly sauté the cauliflower rice for 3–4 minutes, until tender. Season with a pinch of salt and pepper.
6. Serve the beef stroganoff over the cauliflower rice and garnish with fresh parsley.

Serving Suggestions:
For extra vegetables, serve with a side of steamed green beans or peas.

Nutritional Information (Per Serving):
Calories: 330 kcal | Total Fat: 14 g (Saturated Fat: 4 g) | Cholesterol: 65 mg | Fibre: 5 g | Protein: 36 g

Plant-Based Meals

This chapter is dedicated to the vibrant and nourishing world of plant-based cuisine, featuring vegan and vegetarian dishes that are both satisfying and cholesterol-free. Perfect for anyone looking to embrace a healthier lifestyle or simply add more variety to their meals, these recipes are packed with fibre, vitamins, and plant-based protein, all while delivering delicious flavours.

The Benefits of Plant-Based Eating

Plant-based meals are a fantastic way to support heart health, lower cholesterol levels, and improve overall well-being. Packed with antioxidants, healthy fats, and plant-based proteins, vegan and vegetarian dishes help you meet your daily nutrient needs without compromising on flavour or satisfaction.

Some of the key benefits of plant-based eating include:

- **Rich in Fibre**: Found in vegetables, legumes, and whole grains, fibre helps reduce cholesterol absorption and promotes a healthy digestive system.
- **Low in Saturated Fat**: These recipes avoid animal-based saturated fats, making them ideal for managing cholesterol levels.
- **Packed with Nutrients**: Ingredients like lentils, chickpeas, and leafy greens are loaded with iron, magnesium, and vitamins that support energy and overall health.

Why Plant-Based Meals Are Perfect for a Low-Cholesterol Diet

Since cholesterol is found only in animal products, plant-based meals are naturally cholesterol-free, making them a great option for lowering or maintaining healthy cholesterol levels. Even dishes that include small amounts of cheese or yoghurt are crafted with heart health in mind by using low-fat or plant-based alternatives.

Tips for Enjoying Vegan and Vegetarian Meals

- **Experiment with Spices and Herbs**: Use cumin, turmeric, coriander, and thyme to add depth to your dishes.
- **Include Plant-Based Proteins**: Ingredients like lentils, chickpeas, quinoa, and black beans provide protein to keep you energised and full.
- **Use Whole Grains**: Swap white rice or pasta for wholegrain versions to increase fibre and nutrient content.
- **Don't Forget Healthy Fats**: Incorporate olive oil, avocado, or nuts to enhance flavour and provide essential fats.

A Flexible Approach to Plant-Based Eating

Even if you're not fully vegetarian or vegan, incorporating plant-based meals into your routine can help you reduce cholesterol intake and explore new flavours. These recipes are perfect for meat-free days or as creative additions to your low-cholesterol diet.

With these nourishing recipes, you'll discover how satisfying and flavourful plant-based meals can be. From hearty lentil shepherd's pie to comforting mushroom stroganoff, each dish has been carefully designed to delight your taste buds while supporting your heart health.

Lentil and Sweet Potato Shepherd's Pie

Preparation Time: 10 minutes | **Cooking Time:** 30-35 minutes | **Servings:** 1

Ingredients:
For the Filling:
100g dried green or brown lentils, rinsed
1 small onion, chopped
1 garlic clove, minced
1 carrot, diced
1 celery stick, diced
100g canned chopped tomatoes (no added salt)
1 teaspoon olive oil
½ teaspoon dried thyme
½ teaspoon dried oregano
Salt and black pepper to taste
300ml vegetable stock (low-sodium)
For the Sweet Potato Topping:
150g sweet potato, peeled and diced
1 teaspoon olive oil
Salt and black pepper to taste

Instructions:
1. Boil the diced sweet potato in a pot of water for about 15-20 minutes until tender. Drain and set aside.
2. In a saucepan, heat the olive oil over medium heat. Add the chopped onion and garlic, cooking for 2-3 minutes until softened.
3. Stir in the diced carrot and celery, cooking for another 3-4 minutes. Add the rinsed lentils, canned tomatoes, dried thyme, dried oregano, salt, black pepper, and vegetable stock. Bring to a simmer, then cover and cook for about 20-25 minutes, or until the lentils are tender.
4. While the lentils are cooking, mash the boiled sweet potato with a fork or potato masher. Stir in 1 teaspoon of olive oil and season with salt and black pepper.
5. Preheat the oven to 200°C (180°C fan) or gas mark 6. Once the lentil filling is ready, transfer it to a small baking dish. Spread the mashed sweet potato on top, smoothing it out with a spatula.
6. Bake in the preheated oven for 15-20 minutes, or until the topping is slightly golden and the filling is bubbling.
7. Allow to cool slightly before serving.

Serving Suggestions:
Pair with a refreshing salad of mixed baby spinach, grated carrot, and thinly sliced radish, dressed with a light balsamic vinaigrette.

Nutritional Information (Per Serving):
Calories: 320 kcal | Total Fat: 8 g (Saturated Fat: 1 g) | Cholesterol: 0 mg | Fibre: 12 g | Protein: 16 g

Chickpea and Spinach Curry

Preparation Time: 10 minutes | **Cooking Time:** 20 minutes | **Servings:** 1

Ingredients:
1 can (400 g) chickpeas, drained and rinsed
100 g fresh spinach
1 small onion, chopped
1 garlic clove, minced
1 teaspoon fresh ginger, grated (or ½ teaspoon ground ginger)
1 teaspoon olive oil
1 teaspoon curry powder
½ teaspoon ground cumin
100 g canned chopped tomatoes (no added salt)
100 ml low-sodium vegetable stock
Salt and black pepper to taste
Fresh coriander for garnish (optional)

Instructions:
1. Heat the olive oil in a saucepan over medium heat. Add the chopped onion and cook for 2-3 minutes until softened.
2. Stir in the minced garlic and grated ginger, cooking for another minute until fragrant.
3. Add the curry powder and ground cumin, stirring well to coat the onions.
4. Add the canned chopped tomatoes, drained chickpeas, vegetable stock, salt, and black pepper. Bring to a simmer and cook for 10-15 minutes, allowing the flavours to meld.
5. Stir in the fresh spinach and cook for another 2-3 minutes until wilted.
6. Serve warm, garnished with fresh coriander if desired.

Serving Suggestions:
Enjoy with a warm wholemeal chapati or flatbread to scoop up the curry.

Nutritional Information (Per Serving):
Calories: 300 kcal | Total Fat: 8 g (Saturated Fat: 1 g) | Cholesterol: 0 mg | Fibre: 12 g | Protein: 14 g

Butternut Squash Risotto

Preparation Time: 10 minutes | **Cooking Time:** 25-30 minutes | **Servings:** 1

Ingredients:
75 g Arborio rice
150 g butternut squash, peeled and diced
1 small onion, finely chopped
1 garlic clove, minced
1 teaspoon olive oil
500 ml low-sodium vegetable stock, kept warm
1 teaspoon dried thyme (or 1 tablespoon fresh thyme, chopped)
Salt and black pepper to taste
1 tablespoon nutritional yeast (optional, for a cheesy flavour)
Fresh parsley for garnish (optional)

Instructions:
1. In a saucepan, heat the olive oil over medium heat. Add the chopped onion and cook for 2-3 minutes until softened.
2. Stir in the minced garlic and cook for another minute until fragrant.
3. Add the diced butternut squash and cook for about 5 minutes, stirring occasionally.
4. Stir in the Arborio rice, ensuring it is well coated with the oil. Cook for 1-2 minutes until the rice is slightly translucent.
5. Begin adding the warm vegetable stock, one ladleful at a time, stirring frequently. Allow the liquid to be absorbed before adding the next ladleful.
6. After about 15 minutes, add the dried thyme, salt, and black pepper. Continue adding stock and stirring until the rice is creamy and cooked al dente, about 25-30 minutes total.
7. If using, stir in the nutritional yeast for added flavour.
8. Serve warm, garnished with fresh parsley if desired.

Serving Suggestions:
Sprinkle the risotto with roasted pumpkin or sunflower seeds for added crunch and a boost of healthy fats.

Nutritional Information (Per Serving):
Calories: 320 kcal | Total Fat: 7 g (Saturated Fat: 1 g) | Cholesterol: 0 mg | Fibre: 6 g | Protein: 8 g

Mushroom Stroganoff with Wholegrain Pasta

Preparation Time: 10 minutes | **Cooking Time:** 20 minutes | **Servings:** 1

Ingredients:
75 g wholegrain pasta
150 g mushrooms, sliced (such as chestnut or button mushrooms)
1 small onion, finely chopped
1 garlic clove, minced
1 teaspoon olive oil
1 teaspoon Dijon mustard
100 ml low-fat natural yoghurt or plant-based alternative
½ teaspoon dried thyme
Salt and black pepper to taste
Fresh parsley for garnish (optional)

Instructions:
1. Cook the wholegrain pasta according to the package instructions. Drain and set aside.
2. In a saucepan, heat the olive oil over medium heat. Add the chopped onion and cook for 2-3 minutes until softened.
3. Stir in the minced garlic and sliced mushrooms, cooking for another 5-7 minutes until the mushrooms are tender and browned.
4. Add the Dijon mustard, dried thyme, salt, and black pepper. Stir well to combine.
5. Remove the saucepan from the heat and mix in the low-fat natural yoghurt or plant-based alternative until creamy.
6. Combine the mushroom mixture with the cooked wholegrain pasta, mixing well to coat.
7. Serve warm, garnished with fresh parsley if desired.

Serving Suggestions:
Serve alongside steamed broccoli, green beans, or tenderstem broccoli for added nutrients and colour.

Nutritional Information (Per Serving):
Calories: 320 kcal | Total Fat: 7 g (Saturated Fat: 1 g) | Cholesterol: 5 mg | Fibre: 8 g | Protein: 12 g

Cauliflower Steaks with Chimichurri Sauce

Preparation Time: 10 minutes | **Cooking Time:** 20 minutes | **Servings:** 1

Ingredients:
1 medium cauliflower
1 tablespoon olive oil
Salt and black pepper to taste
For the Chimichurri Sauce:
2 tablespoons fresh parsley, chopped
1 tablespoon fresh coriander, chopped
1 garlic clove, minced
1 teaspoon red wine vinegar
1 teaspoon olive oil
½ teaspoon dried oregano
Salt and black pepper to taste

Instructions:
1. Preheat the oven to 200°C (180°C fan) or gas mark 6.
2. Remove the leaves from the cauliflower and slice it into thick steaks (about 2-3 cm each).
3. Brush both sides of the cauliflower steaks with olive oil and season with salt and black pepper.
4. Place the cauliflower steaks on a baking sheet lined with parchment paper and bake in the preheated oven for 20 minutes, flipping halfway through, until golden and tender.
5. While the cauliflower is baking, prepare the chimichurri sauce by combining the chopped parsley, coriander, minced garlic, red wine vinegar, olive oil, dried oregano, salt, and black pepper in a small bowl. Mix well.
6. Once the cauliflower steaks are cooked, remove them from the oven and serve warm, drizzled with chimichurri sauce.

Serving Suggestions:
Top the steaks with a fresh tomato salsa made with diced tomatoes, red onion, and lime juice for a zesty twist.

Nutritional Information (Per Serving):
Calories: 220 kcal | Total Fat: 12 g (Saturated Fat: 1.5 g) | Cholesterol: 0 mg | Fibre: 7 g | Protein: 4 g

Spinach and Feta Stuffed Portobello Mushrooms

Preparation Time: 10 minutes | **Cooking Time:** 20 minutes | **Servings:** 1

Ingredients:
2 large portobello mushrooms
100 g fresh spinach, chopped
50 g feta cheese, crumbled
1 garlic clove, minced
1 teaspoon olive oil
1 teaspoon dried oregano
Salt and black pepper to taste
Fresh parsley for garnish (optional)

Instructions:
1. Preheat the oven to 200°C (180°C fan) or gas mark 6.
2. Gently clean the portobello mushrooms with a damp cloth and remove the stems. Place them, cap side up, on a baking sheet lined with parchment paper.
3. In a pan, heat the olive oil over medium heat. Add the minced garlic and cook for 1 minute until fragrant.
4. Stir in the chopped spinach and cook for 2-3 minutes until wilted. Remove from heat and let cool slightly.
5. In a bowl, combine the cooked spinach, crumbled feta cheese, dried oregano, salt, and black pepper. Mix well to combine.
6. Spoon the spinach and feta mixture into the mushroom caps, pressing down gently to pack the filling.
7. Bake the stuffed mushrooms in the preheated oven for 15-20 minutes, or until the mushrooms are tender and the filling is heated through.
8. Remove from the oven and garnish with fresh parsley if desired. Serve warm.

Serving Suggestions:
Place the mushrooms on a salad of peppery rocket and roasted beetroot, drizzled with balsamic glaze.

Nutritional Information (Per Serving):
Calories: 230 kcal | Total Fat: 12 g (Saturated Fat: 5 g) | Cholesterol: 20 mg | Fibre: 3 g | Protein: 14 g

Spinach and Tomato Pasta with Chickpeas

Preparation Time: 10 minutes | **Cooking Time:** 15 minutes | **Servings:** 1

Ingredients:
75 g wholewheat pasta
100 g fresh spinach, roughly chopped
100 g canned chopped tomatoes (no added salt)
100 g canned chickpeas, drained and rinsed
1 small onion, finely chopped
1 garlic clove, minced
1 teaspoon olive oil
½ teaspoon dried oregano
Salt and black pepper to taste
Fresh basil for garnish (optional)

Instructions:
1. Cook the wholewheat pasta according to the package instructions. Drain and set aside.
2. In a saucepan, heat the olive oil over medium heat. Add the chopped onion and cook for 2-3 minutes until softened.
3. Stir in the minced garlic and cook for another minute until fragrant.
4. Add the canned chopped tomatoes, chickpeas, dried oregano, salt, and black pepper. Bring to a simmer and cook for about 5 minutes until heated through.
5. Stir in the fresh spinach and cook for another 2-3 minutes until wilted.
6. Combine the cooked pasta with the tomato and chickpea mixture, mixing well to coat.
7. Serve warm, garnished with fresh basil if desired.

Serving Suggestions:
Sprinkle with toasted wholegrain breadcrumbs mixed with a pinch of chilli flakes and garlic powder for added crunch.

Nutritional Information (Per Serving):
Calories: 350 kcal | Total Fat: 8 g (Saturated Fat: 1 g) | Cholesterol: 0 mg | Fibre: 12 g | Protein: 15 g

Stuffed Sweet Peppers with Quinoa and Black Beans

Preparation Time: 10 minutes | **Cooking Time:** 30-35 minutes | **Servings:** 1

Ingredients:
1 large sweet pepper
75 g quinoa, rinsed
100 g canned black beans, drained and rinsed
1 small onion, chopped
1 garlic clove, minced
1 teaspoon olive oil
100 g canned chopped tomatoes (no added salt)
½ teaspoon cumin
½ teaspoon smoked paprika
Salt and black pepper to taste
Fresh coriander for garnish (optional)

Instructions:
1. Preheat the oven to 200°C (180°C fan) or gas mark 6.
2. Cook the quinoa according to the package instructions and set aside.
3. In a pan, heat the olive oil over medium heat. Add the chopped onion and cook for 2-3 minutes until softened.
4. Stir in the minced garlic and cook for another minute until fragrant.
5. Add the canned chopped tomatoes, black beans, cooked quinoa, cumin, smoked paprika, salt, and black pepper. Mix well and cook for another 2-3 minutes until heated through.
6. Cut the top off the sweet pepper and remove the seeds and membranes. Stuff the pepper with the quinoa and bean mixture, packing it down gently.
7. Place the stuffed sweet pepper in a baking dish and bake in the preheated oven for 30-35 minutes, or until the pepper is tender.
8. Remove from the oven and garnish with fresh coriander if desired. Serve warm.

Serving Suggestions:
Add a spoonful of fresh tomato salsa or pico de gallo on top of the stuffed pepper for an extra layer of freshness.

Nutritional Information (Per Serving):
Calories: 320 kcal | Total Fat: 6 g (Saturated Fat: 1 g) | Cholesterol: 0 mg | Fibre: 10 g | Protein: 14 g

Roasted Vegetable and Hummus Wrap

Preparation Time: 10 minutes | **Cooking Time:** 20 minutes | **Servings:** 1

Ingredients:
1 wholemeal wrap
100 g mixed vegetables (such as sweet peppers, courgettes, and aubergine), chopped
1 teaspoon olive oil
Salt and black pepper to taste
2 tablespoons hummus
Handful of fresh spinach or salad leaves
1 teaspoon balsamic vinegar (optional)

Instructions:
1. Preheat the oven to 200°C (180°C fan) or gas mark 6.
2. In a bowl, toss the chopped mixed vegetables with olive oil, salt, and black pepper until evenly coated.
3. Spread the vegetables on a baking tray lined with parchment paper and roast in the preheated oven for about 20 minutes, or until tender and slightly caramelised.
4. Once the vegetables are roasted, remove them from the oven and allow them to cool slightly.
5. Spread the hummus evenly over the wholemeal wrap.
6. Layer the roasted vegetables and fresh spinach or salad leaves on top of the hummus.
7. Drizzle with balsamic vinegar if desired.
8. Roll the wrap tightly, slice in half, and serve.

Serving Suggestions:
Add falafel inside the wrap for an additional layer of texture and protein.

Nutritional Information (Per Serving):
Calories: 320 kcal | Total Fat: 9 g (Saturated Fat: 1 g) | Cholesterol: 0 mg | Fibre: 8 g | Protein: 10 g

Thai Peanut Buddha Bowl

Preparation Time: 15 minutes | **Cooking Time:** 15 minutes | **Servings:** 1

Ingredients:
75 g brown rice or quinoa
100 g mixed vegetables (such as carrots, sweet peppers, and cucumber), chopped
50 g edamame beans (fresh or frozen)
Handful of fresh spinach or salad leaves
1 tablespoon natural peanut butter (no added sugar)
1 tablespoon soy sauce (low sodium)
1 teaspoon lime juice
1 teaspoon sesame oil (optional)
1 teaspoon fresh coriander, chopped (for garnish)

Instructions:
1. Cook the brown rice or quinoa according to the package instructions. Set aside when done.
2. In a pan, lightly steam the mixed vegetables until tender, about 5-7 minutes. If using frozen edamame, add them during the last few minutes of cooking to heat through.
3. In a small bowl, whisk together the natural peanut butter, soy sauce, lime juice, and sesame oil until smooth.
4. In a serving bowl, layer the cooked rice or quinoa, steamed vegetables, edamame, and fresh spinach or salad leaves.
5. Drizzle the Thai peanut sauce over the top and toss gently to combine.
6. Garnish with fresh coriander if desired. Serve warm or at room temperature.

Serving Suggestions:
Add slices of fresh mango or pineapple for a sweet, tropical twist.

Nutritional Information (Per Serving):
Calories: 400 kcal | Total Fat: 16 g (Saturated Fat: 2 g) | Cholesterol: 0 mg | Fibre: 10 g | Protein: 15 g

Vegan Lentil Bolognese

Preparation Time: 10 minutes | **Cooking Time:** 30 minutes | **Servings:** 1

Ingredients:
75 g dried green or brown lentils, rinsed
1 small onion, finely chopped
1 carrot, diced
1 celery stick, diced
2 garlic cloves, minced
100 g canned chopped tomatoes (no added salt)
1 teaspoon olive oil
½ teaspoon dried oregano
½ teaspoon dried basil
200 ml vegetable stock (low sodium)
Salt and black pepper to taste
75 g wholewheat pasta
Fresh basil for garnish (optional)

Instructions:
1. Cook the wholewheat pasta according to the package instructions. Drain and set aside.
2. In a saucepan, heat the olive oil over medium heat. Add the chopped onion, carrot, and celery, cooking for 5-7 minutes until softened.
3. Stir in the minced garlic and cook for another minute until fragrant.
4. Add the rinsed lentils, canned chopped tomatoes, dried oregano, dried basil, vegetable stock, salt, and black pepper. Bring to a simmer.
5. Cover and cook for about 25 minutes, or until the lentils are tender and the sauce has thickened. Stir occasionally and add a little water if needed.
6. Serve the lentil bolognese over the cooked pasta and garnish with fresh basil if desired.

Serving Suggestions:
Pair with slices of wholegrain garlic bread brushed lightly with olive oil and minced garlic for a classic accompaniment.

Nutritional Information (Per Serving):
Calories: 360 kcal | Total Fat: 6 g (Saturated Fat: 1 g) | Cholesterol: 0 mg | Fibre: 15 g | Protein: 20 g

Courgette Noodles with Pesto and Cherry Tomatoes

Preparation Time: 10 minutes | **Cooking Time:** 5 minutes | **Servings:** 1

Ingredients:
1 large courgette, spiralised into noodles
100 g cherry tomatoes, halved
1 tablespoon pesto (store-bought or homemade)
1 teaspoon olive oil
Salt and black pepper to taste
Fresh basil for garnish (optional)

Instructions:
1. In a pan, heat the olive oil over medium heat. Add the halved cherry tomatoes and cook for about 2-3 minutes until they begin to soften.
2. Add the spiralised courgette noodles to the pan and cook for another 2-3 minutes, stirring gently until the courgette is just tender but still retains some crunch.
3. Remove the pan from the heat and stir in the pesto until the courgette noodles and tomatoes are well coated. Season with salt and black pepper to taste.
4. Serve warm, garnished with fresh basil if desired.

Serving Suggestions:
Pair with grilled tofu slices seasoned with Italian herbs for a protein-packed vegan option.

Nutritional Information (Per Serving):
Calories: 220 kcal | Total Fat: 10 g (Saturated Fat: 1.5 g) | Cholesterol: 0 mg | Fibre: 5 g | Protein: 5 g

Spinach and Feta Dumplings

Preparation Time: 15 minutes | **Cooking Time:** 15 minutes | **Servings:** 1

Ingredients:

For the Dumpling Dough:

100g plain wholemeal flour
30ml water
A pinch of salt

For the Filling:

50g fresh spinach, chopped
25g feta cheese, crumbled
1 garlic clove, minced
Salt and black pepper to taste

Instructions:

1. In a bowl, combine the plain wholemeal flour and a pinch of salt. Gradually add the water, mixing until a dough forms. Knead for a couple of minutes until smooth, then cover with a damp cloth and set aside.
2. In a pan, lightly sauté the minced garlic in a small amount of water or olive oil for 1-2 minutes until fragrant. Add the chopped spinach and cook until wilted, about 2-3 minutes. Remove from heat and let cool slightly. In a bowl, combine the cooked spinach and feta cheese, seasoning with salt and black pepper.
3. Divide the dough into small pieces (about the size of a golf ball). Roll each piece into a circle, approximately 5 cm (about 2 inches) in diameter. Place a spoonful of the spinach and feta mixture in the centre of each wrapper. Fold the dough over the filling and pinch the edges to seal, ensuring no filling escapes.
4. Bring a pot of water to a gentle simmer. Carefully add the dumplings to the water and cook for about 5-7 minutes until they float to the surface and are cooked through.
5. Remove the dumplings with a slotted spoon and serve warm, optionally drizzled with a little olive oil or a sprinkle of fresh herbs.

Serving Suggestions:

Pair with a homemade tzatziki sauce made from cucumber, mint, and low-fat yoghurt for a Greek-inspired option.

Nutritional Information (Per Serving):

Calories: 320 kcal | Total Fat: 10 g (Saturated Fat: 3 g) | Cholesterol: 10 mg | Fibre: 4 g | Protein: 12 g

Spicy Quinoa and Black Bean Burger

Preparation Time: 10 minutes | **Cooking Time:** 20-25 minutes | **Servings:** 1

Ingredients:

50 g cooked quinoa
100 g canned black beans, drained and rinsed
1 small onion, finely chopped
1 garlic clove, minced
½ teaspoon cumin
½ teaspoon smoked paprika
½ teaspoon chilli powder (adjust to taste)
1 tablespoon wholemeal flour (or oat flour)
Salt and black pepper to taste
Wholemeal bun
Fresh salad leaves and tomato slices

Instructions:

1. Preheat the oven to 200°C (180°C fan) or gas mark 6. Line a baking tray with parchment paper.
2. In a bowl, mash the black beans with a fork until mostly smooth, leaving some chunks for texture.
3. Add the cooked quinoa, chopped onion, minced garlic, cumin, smoked paprika, chilli powder, wholemeal flour, salt, and black pepper. Mix well to combine.
4. Form the mixture into a patty, pressing firmly to hold its shape.
5. Place the patty on the lined baking tray.
6. Bake in the preheated oven for 20-25 minutes, flipping halfway through, until golden brown and heated through.
7. Serve the spicy quinoa and black bean burger in a wholemeal bun, topped with fresh salad leaves and tomato slices if desired.

Serving Suggestions:

Top the burger with a dollop of guacamole for a creamy and flavourful twist.

Nutritional Information (Per Serving):

Calories: 300 kcal | Total Fat: 5 g (Saturated Fat: 0.5 g) | Cholesterol: 0 mg | Fibre: 10 g | Protein: 15 g

Chickpea and Butternut Squash Tagine

Preparation Time: 15 minutes | **Cooking Time:** 35-40 minutes | **Servings:** 1

Ingredients:
1/2 tbsp olive oil
1 small onion, chopped
1 garlic clove, minced
1/4 butternut squash, peeled and diced
1/2 can (200 g) chickpeas, drained and rinsed
1/2 tsp ground cumin
1/2 tsp ground coriander
1/4 tsp ground turmeric
1/4 tsp cinnamon
1/4 tsp ground ginger
1/2 tbsp tomato purée
200 ml vegetable stock (low-sodium)
1/4 cup dried apricots, chopped
1/2 tbsp fresh coriander, chopped (for garnish)
Salt and pepper, to taste

Instructions:
1. Heat the olive oil in a large pan over medium heat. Add the onion and cook for 5 minutes until softened.
2. Add the garlic, butternut squash, and spices (cumin, coriander, turmeric, cinnamon, and ginger). Stir to coat the vegetables and cook for 2–3 minutes.
3. Stir in the tomato purée, chickpeas, apricots, and vegetable stock. Bring to a simmer and cover the pan. Cook for 30–35 minutes, until the squash is tender and the flavours have melded.
4. Season with salt and pepper to taste, and garnish with fresh coriander.

Serving Suggestions:
Pair with a side of steamed greens such as spinach or kale.

Nutritional Information (Per Serving):
Calories: 320 kcal | Total Fat: 9 g (Saturated Fat: 1 g) | Cholesterol: 0 mg | Fibre: 12 g | Protein: 12 g

Spicy Lentil and Cauliflower Stew

Preparation Time: 10 minutes | **Cooking Time:** 30 minutes | **Servings:** 1

Ingredients:
1/2 tbsp olive oil
1/2 small onion, chopped
1 garlic clove, minced
1/2 small cauliflower, cut into florets
1/2 cup dried red lentils, rinsed
1/2 can (200 g) diced tomatoes
1/2 tsp ground cumin
1/4 tsp ground paprika
1/4 tsp cayenne pepper (optional)
1/2 tsp ground turmeric
250 ml vegetable stock (low-sodium)
1/2 tbsp fresh lemon juice
Fresh parsley, chopped (for garnish)
Salt and pepper, to taste

Instructions:
1. Heat the olive oil in a large pot over medium heat. Add the onion and cook for 5 minutes until softened.
2. Add the garlic, cauliflower florets, and spices (cumin, paprika, cayenne, and turmeric). Stir to coat and cook for 2 minutes.
3. Add the red lentils, diced tomatoes, and vegetable stock. Bring to a simmer, cover the pot, and cook for 25–30 minutes, until the lentils are tender and the stew has thickened.
4. Stir in the lemon juice, then season with salt and pepper to taste. Garnish with fresh parsley before serving.

Serving Suggestions:
Pair with a fresh cucumber and tomato salad for a refreshing contrast.

Nutritional Information (Per Serving):
Calories: 280 kcal | Total Fat: 7 g (Saturated Fat: 1 g) | Cholesterol: 0 mg | Fibre: 14 g | Protein: 18 g

Snacks and Light Bites

Snacks and light bites are essential for keeping hunger at bay and maintaining energy throughout the day. Whether you're looking for a quick pick-me-up between meals or something to satisfy your cravings, this chapter is packed with delicious and healthy options to suit any occasion.

Why Snacks Matter in a Low-Cholesterol Diet
Snacking doesn't have to derail your healthy eating goals. In fact, choosing heart-friendly snacks can help you stay on track with a low-cholesterol lifestyle. Snacks rich in fibre, healthy fats, and plant-based ingredients can support cholesterol management and provide a boost of energy between meals.

Some of the benefits of mindful snacking include:
- **Steady Energy Levels**: Snacks with complex carbohydrates, protein, and healthy fats provide sustained energy throughout the day.
- **Heart-Healthy Ingredients**: Incorporating ingredients like oats, nuts, seeds, and vegetables can aid in cholesterol reduction and support heart health.
- **Portion Control**: Preparing snacks at home allows you to manage portions and avoid unnecessary added sugars, salts, and unhealthy fats often found in processed options.

Tips for Snacking Smart
- **Plan Ahead**: Prepare snacks in advance so you have healthy options on hand when cravings hit.
- **Focus on Whole Foods**: Choose minimally processed ingredients, such as fruits, vegetables, and whole grains, for maximum nutrients.
- **Incorporate Protein and Fibre**: These nutrients help keep you fuller for longer and prevent overeating later in the day.
- **Pair Snacks with Drinks**: Enjoy your snacks with a calming herbal tea, a refreshing glass of water, or a plant-based milk alternative.

Embracing Variety and Balance
This collection of snacks and light bites ranges from savoury to sweet, crunchy to creamy, ensuring there's something for every taste. These recipes are simple to prepare, delicious, and tailored to a low-cholesterol lifestyle.

From crisp courgette chips to hearty oat biscuits, you'll find snacks that are not only nourishing but also satisfying. The key to successful snacking is balance—combine nutrient-dense foods like vegetables, nuts, and legumes with flavours you love.

With these recipes, you'll see that snacks can be both indulgent and health-conscious, proving that a low-cholesterol diet is anything but boring.

Oat Biscuits with Raisins and Nuts

Preparation Time: 10 minutes | **Cooking Time:** 15-20 minutes | **Servings:** 12 biscuits

Ingredients:
100 g wholemeal flour
100 g rolled oats
50 g raisins
50 g mixed nuts (such as almonds and walnuts), chopped
50 g soft brown sugar (or coconut sugar)
1 teaspoon baking powder
1 teaspoon cinnamon
1 pinch of salt
60 ml unsweetened apple sauce (for moisture)
20 ml vegetable oil (such as sunflower or canola)
1 teaspoon vanilla extract

Instructions:
1. Preheat the oven to 180°C (160°C fan) or gas mark 4. Line a baking tray with parchment paper.
2. In a large bowl, mix the wholemeal flour, rolled oats, raisins, chopped nuts, brown sugar, baking powder, cinnamon, and salt until well combined.
3. In a separate bowl, whisk together the apple sauce, vegetable oil, and vanilla extract until smooth.
4. Pour the wet ingredients into the dry ingredients and mix until just combined. The mixture should be slightly sticky.
5. Using a spoon or your hands, scoop out small amounts of the mixture and form into balls. Place them on the prepared baking tray, flattening each ball slightly to form a biscuit shape.
6. Bake in the preheated oven for 15-20 minutes, or until the biscuits are golden brown and firm to the touch.
7. Remove from the oven and allow to cool on the tray for a few minutes before transferring to a wire rack to cool completely.

Serving Suggestions:
Serve the biscuits with a warm cup of black tea, green tea, or herbal infusion for a classic British pairing.

Nutritional Information (Per Serving):
Calories: 100 kcal | Total Fat: 4 g (Saturated Fat: 0.5 g) | Cholesterol: 0 mg | Fibre: 2 g | Protein: 3 g

Courgette Chips with Herbs

Preparation Time: 10 minutes | **Cooking Time:** 20-25 minutes | **Servings:** 1

Ingredients:
1 large courgette, thinly sliced
1 tablespoon olive oil
½ teaspoon dried oregano
½ teaspoon dried thyme
Salt and black pepper to taste

Instructions:
1. Preheat the oven to 200°C (180°C fan) or gas mark 6. Line a baking tray with parchment paper.
2. In a bowl, combine the thinly sliced courgette with olive oil, dried oregano, dried thyme, salt, and black pepper. Toss until the courgette slices are evenly coated.
3. Spread the courgette slices in a single layer on the prepared baking tray, ensuring they do not overlap.
4. Bake in the preheated oven for 25-30 minutes, or until the courgette chips are crispy and golden, flipping them halfway through to ensure even cooking.
5. Remove from the oven and let cool slightly before serving. Enjoy your courgette chips warm or at room temperature.

Serving Suggestions:
Serve alongside hummus, guacamole, or a light salsa for a flavourful snack

Nutritional Information (Per Serving):
Calories: 120 kcal | Total Fat: 7 g (Saturated Fat: 1 g) | Cholesterol: 0 mg | Fibre: 3 g | Protein: 2 g

Cucumber Rounds with Tzatziki

Preparation Time: 10 minutes | **Servings:** 1

Ingredients:
1 medium cucumber, sliced into rounds
100 g low-fat natural yoghurt (or plant-based yoghurt)
1 garlic clove, minced
1 teaspoon fresh dill, chopped (or ½ teaspoon dried dill)
Juice of ½ lemon
Salt and black pepper to taste

Instructions:
1. In a bowl, combine the low-fat natural yoghurt, minced garlic, chopped dill, lemon juice, salt, and black pepper. Mix well until smooth.
2. Arrange the cucumber rounds on a serving plate.
3. Spoon a small amount of the tzatziki mixture onto each cucumber round.
4. Serve immediately as a refreshing snack or light bite.

Serving Suggestions:
Add a small slice of smoked salmon on top of the tzatziki for an elegant appetiser.

Nutritional Information (Per Serving):
Calories: 80 kcal | Total Fat: 2 g (Saturated Fat: 0.5 g) | Cholesterol: 5 mg | Fibre: 1 g | Protein: 4 g

Roasted Cauliflower Bites with Garlic Dip

Preparation Time: 10 minutes | **Cooking Time:** 25 minutes | **Servings:** 1

Ingredients:
200g cauliflower, cut into bite-sized florets
1 tablespoon olive oil
½ teaspoon smoked paprika
Salt and black pepper to taste

For the Garlic Dip:
100g low-fat natural yoghurt
1 garlic clove, minced
1 teaspoon lemon juice
Salt and black pepper to taste

Instructions:
1. Preheat the oven to 200°C (180°C fan) or gas mark 6. Line a baking tray with parchment paper.
2. In a bowl, toss the cauliflower florets with olive oil, smoked paprika, salt, and black pepper until well coated.
3. Spread the cauliflower bites in a single layer on the prepared baking tray.
4. Roast in the preheated oven for 25 minutes, or until golden brown and tender, turning halfway through cooking.
5. While the cauliflower is roasting, prepare the garlic dip by combining the low-fat natural yoghurt, minced garlic, lemon juice, salt, and black pepper in a bowl. Mix well until smooth.
6. Once the cauliflower bites are cooked, remove them from the oven and serve warm with the garlic dip on the side.

Serving Suggestions:
Serve alongside wholemeal crackers for scooping up the garlic dip and cauliflower bites.

Nutritional Information (Per Serving):
Calories: 180 kcal | Total Fat: 8 g (Saturated Fat: 1 g) | Cholesterol: 0 mg | Fibre: 4 g | Protein: 6 g

Apple Slices with Nut Butter

Preparation Time: 5 minutes | **Cooking Time:** 0 minutes | **Servings:** 1

Ingredients:
1 medium apple, sliced
2 tablespoons nut butter (such as almond butter or peanut butter, no added sugar)
A sprinkle of cinnamon (optional)

Instructions:
1. Wash the apple thoroughly and slice it into rounds or wedges, removing the core as needed.
2. Arrange the apple slices on a plate.
3. Spread the nut butter evenly over the apple slices.
4. If desired, sprinkle a little cinnamon on top for added flavour.

Serving Suggestions:
Serve alongside fresh raspberries, blueberries, or strawberries for a refreshing snack.

Nutritional Information (Per Serving):
Calories: 250 kcal | Total Fat: 16 g (Saturated Fat: 2 g) | Cholesterol: 0 mg | Fibre: 5 g | Protein: 6 g

Baked Beetroot Crisps

Preparation Time: 10 minutes | **Cooking Time:** 30-35 minutes | **Servings:** 1

Ingredients:
200 g beetroot, peeled and thinly sliced (using a mandoline is recommended)
1 tablespoon olive oil
Salt and black pepper to taste
½ teaspoon smoked paprika (optional)

Instructions:
1. Preheat the oven to 200°C (180°C fan) or gas mark 6. Line a baking tray with parchment paper.
2. In a bowl, toss the thinly sliced beetroot with olive oil, salt, black pepper, and smoked paprika until evenly coated.
3. Spread the beetroot slices in a single layer on the prepared baking tray, ensuring they do not overlap.
4. Bake in the preheated oven for 30-35 minutes, flipping the slices halfway through, until the crisps are crispy and slightly browned.
5. Remove from the oven and let cool for a few minutes before serving.

Serving Suggestions:
Add a light drizzle of balsamic glaze over the crisps for a touch of sweetness and tang.

Nutritional Information (Per Serving):
Calories: 150 kcal | Total Fat: 7 g (Saturated Fat: 1 g) | Cholesterol: 0 mg | Fibre: 5 g | Protein: 3 g

Herbed Wholemeal Pitta Bread with Baba Ganoush

Preparation Time: 10 minutes | **Cooking Time:** 25-30 minutes | **Servings:** 1

Ingredients:
For the Herbed Wholemeal Pitta Bread:
2 wholemeal pitta breads
1 tablespoon olive oil
1 teaspoon dried oregano
1 teaspoon dried thyme
Salt and black pepper to taste
For the Baba Ganoush:
1 medium aubergine 1 garlic clove, minced
2 tablespoons tahini
1 tablespoon lemon juice
1 tablespoon olive oil
Salt to taste
Fresh parsley for garnish (optional)

Instructions:
1. Preheat the oven to 200°C (180°C fan) or gas mark 6. Prick the aubergine with a fork and place it on a baking tray. Roast for about 25-30 minutes, until the skin is charred, and the flesh is soft. Allow to cool slightly before peeling off the skin.
2. In a bowl, combine the roasted aubergine flesh, minced garlic, tahini, lemon juice, olive oil, and salt. Mash until smooth, adjusting seasoning as needed. Set aside.
3. While the aubergine is roasting, place the pitta breads on another baking tray. Brush both sides with olive oil and sprinkle with dried oregano, dried thyme, salt, and black pepper.
4. Bake the pitta breads in the oven for 5-7 minutes, or until warmed and slightly crispy.
5. Cut the herbed pitta breads into triangles and serve warm with the baba ganoush, garnished with fresh parsley if desired.

Serving Suggestions:
Sprinkle the baba ganoush with pomegranate seeds for a pop of colour and a sweet-tangy contrast.

Nutritional Information (Per Serving):
Calories: 180 kcal | Total Fat: 7 g (Saturated Fat: 1 g) | Cholesterol: 0 mg | Fibre: 6 g | Protein: 8 g

Hummus

Preparation Time: 10 minutes | **Cooking Time:** 0 minutes | **Servings:** 4

Ingredients:
1 can (400 g) chickpeas, drained and rinsed
2 tablespoons tahini
1 garlic clove, minced
Juice of 1 lemon
2 tablespoons olive oil
½ teaspoon ground cumin
Salt to taste
Water (as needed for consistency)

Instructions:
1. In a food processor, combine the drained chickpeas, tahini, minced garlic, lemon juice, olive oil, ground cumin, and salt.
2. Blend until smooth, adding water a tablespoon at a time as needed to achieve your desired consistency.
3. Taste and adjust seasoning if necessary, adding more salt or lemon juice as desired.
4. Transfer the hummus to a serving bowl and drizzle a little olive oil on top for garnish if desired.

Serving Suggestions:
Pair with crunchy carrot sticks, cucumber batons, celery sticks, and cherry tomatoes for a refreshing, healthy snack.

Nutritional Information (Per Serving):
Calories: 80 kcal | Total Fat: 4 g (Saturated Fat: 0.5 g) | Cholesterol: 0 mg | Fibre: 2 g | Protein: 4 g

Cucumber and Avocado Bites

Preparation Time: 10 minutes | **Cooking Time:** 0 minutes | **Servings:** 1

Ingredients:
1 small cucumber
½ ripe avocado
1 small tomato, diced
1 teaspoon lemon juice
1 teaspoon fresh parsley, chopped
A pinch of smoked paprika (optional)
Salt and black pepper to taste

Instructions:
1. Slice the cucumber into thick rounds.
2. In a small bowl, mash the avocado with a fork. Stir in the lemon juice, salt, and black pepper to taste.
3. Top each cucumber round with a spoonful of the mashed avocado.
4. Sprinkle the diced tomato over the avocado-topped cucumber slices.
5. Garnish with chopped parsley and a pinch of smoked paprika, if using.
6. Serve immediately as a refreshing, light snack.

Serving Suggestions:
Replace or complement the parsley with finely chopped fresh mint for a refreshing flavour.

Nutritional Information (Per Serving):
Calories: 120 kcal | Total Fat: 80 g (Saturated Fat: 1.5 g) | Cholesterol: 0 mg | Fibre: 4 g | Protein: 2 g

Chicken and Vegetable Lettuce Wraps

Preparation Time: 10 minutes | **Cooking Time:** 15-20 minutes | **Servings:** 1

Ingredients:
150 g skinless chicken breast, minced
1 small onion, finely chopped
1 garlic clove, minced
1 carrot, grated
1 red bell pepper, finely chopped
1 tablespoon low-sodium soy sauce
1 teaspoon fresh ginger, grated
4-6 large lettuce leaves (such as iceberg or romaine)
Fresh coriander for garnish (optional)

Instructions:
1. Preheat the oven to 200°C (180°C fan) or gas mark 6.
2. In a large bowl, combine the minced chicken, chopped onion, minced garlic, grated carrot, chopped red bell pepper, soy sauce, and grated ginger. Mix well to combine.
3. Spread the mixture evenly on a lined baking tray.
4. Bake in the preheated oven for 15-20 minutes, stirring halfway through, until the chicken is fully cooked and the vegetables are tender.
5. Remove from the oven and allow to cool slightly.
6. To serve, spoon the chicken and vegetable mixture into the large lettuce leaves. Garnish with fresh coriander if desired.

Serving Suggestions:
Top with a light peanut dressing made from low-sodium peanut butter, soy sauce, lime juice, and a splash of water for a satay-style twist.

Nutritional Information (Per Serving):
Calories: 200 kcal | Total Fat: 5 g (Saturated Fat: 1 g) | Cholesterol: 75 mg | Fibre: 3 g | Protein: 30 g

Stuffed Tomatoes with Quinoa

Preparation Time: 10 minutes | **Cooking Time:** 25 minutes | **Servings:** 1

Ingredients:
2 large ripe tomatoes
1/4 cup quinoa, rinsed
1/2 tsp olive oil
1 small garlic clove, minced
1/4 small onion, chopped
1/4 cup cooked chickpeas (optional)
1 tbsp fresh basil, chopped
1 tbsp fresh parsley, chopped
1/2 tsp ground cumin
Salt and pepper, to taste
1 tbsp lemon juice

Instructions:
1. Preheat the oven to 180°C (160°C fan) or 350°F.
2. Cut the tops off the tomatoes and carefully scoop out the insides with a spoon, discarding the seeds and excess juice. Set the hollowed tomatoes aside.
3. Cook the quinoa according to package instructions, usually about 15 minutes. Once cooked, fluff with a fork and set aside.
4. Heat the olive oil in a small pan over medium heat. Add the garlic and onion and cook for 3–4 minutes until softened.
5. Add the cooked quinoa, chickpeas (if using), fresh basil, parsley, ground cumin, salt, and pepper to the pan. Stir to combine and cook for 2–3 minutes until the flavours meld together.
6. Spoon the quinoa mixture into the hollowed tomatoes, pressing gently to fill them completely.
7. Place the stuffed tomatoes on a baking tray and bake for 20–25 minutes, until the tomatoes are tender.
8. Drizzle with lemon juice and serve hot.

Serving Suggestions:
Pair with a drizzle of tahini or a dollop of Greek yoghurt (low-fat).

Nutritional Information (Per Serving):
Calories: 220 kcal | Total Fat: 5 g (Saturated Fat: 1 g) | Cholesterol: 0 mg | Fibre: 7 g | Protein: 8 g

Smashed Avocado and Tomato Bruschetta

Preparation Time: 10 minutes | **Cooking Time:** 5-7 minutes | **Servings:** 1

Ingredients:
1 ripe avocado
2 small tomatoes, diced
1 tablespoon fresh basil, chopped
1 teaspoon lemon juice
Salt and black pepper to taste
2 slices wholemeal bread
1 teaspoon olive oil

Instructions:
1. In a bowl, mash the ripe avocado with a fork. Stir in the diced tomatoes, chopped basil, lemon juice, salt, and black pepper until well combined.
2. Preheat the oven to 200°C (180°C fan) or gas mark 6.
3. Lightly brush the wholemeal bread slices with olive oil on both sides.
4. Place the bread slices on a baking tray and toast them in the oven for 5-7 minutes, or until golden brown and crispy.
5. Once toasted, remove the bread from the oven and top each slice with the smashed avocado and tomato mixture.
6. Serve immediately as a light snack or appetiser.

Serving Suggestions:
Add a pinch of chilli flakes for a spicy twist to balance the creamy avocado.

Nutritional Information (Per Serving):
Calories: 280 kcal | Total Fat: 15 g (Saturated Fat: 2 g) | Cholesterol: 0 mg | Fibre: 8 g | Protein: 6 g

Oven-Baked Falafel Balls

Preparation Time: 15 minutes | **Cooking Time:** 20-25 minutes | **Servings:** 1

Ingredients:
200 g canned chickpeas, drained and rinsed
1 small onion, finely chopped
2 garlic cloves, minced
1 tablespoon fresh parsley, chopped
1 tablespoon fresh coriander, chopped
1 teaspoon ground cumin
1 teaspoon ground coriander
1 tablespoon wholemeal flour
1 teaspoon baking powder
Salt and black pepper to taste
1 tablespoon olive oil

Instructions:
1. Preheat the oven to 200°C (180°C fan) or gas mark 6. Line a baking tray with parchment paper.
2. In a food processor, combine the drained chickpeas, chopped onion, minced garlic, parsley, coriander, ground cumin, ground coriander, wholemeal flour, baking powder, salt, and black pepper. Blend until the mixture is well combined but still slightly chunky.
3. Using your hands, form small balls (about the size of a golf ball) from the mixture and place them on the prepared baking tray.
4. Drizzle the olive oil over the falafel balls, ensuring they are lightly coated.
5. Bake in the preheated oven for 20-25 minutes, turning halfway through, until golden brown and crisp on the outside.
6. Remove from the oven and allow to cool slightly before serving.

Serving Suggestions:
Serve alongside a simple dip made from tahini, lemon juice, garlic, and a splash of water for a creamy, tangy complement.

Nutritional Information (Per Serving):
Calories: 250 kcal | Total Fat: 8 g (Saturated Fat: 1 g) | Cholesterol: 0 mg | Fibre: 6 g | Protein: 10 g

Crispy Roasted Chickpeas with Spices

Preparation Time: 5 minutes | **Cooking Time:** 20-25 minutes | **Servings:** 1

Ingredients:
1 can (400 g) chickpeas, drained and rinsed
1 tablespoon olive oil
1 teaspoon smoked paprika
½ teaspoon ground cumin
½ teaspoon garlic powder
Salt and black pepper to taste

Instructions:
1. Preheat the oven to 200°C (180°C fan) or gas mark 6. Line a baking tray with parchment paper.
2. Drain and rinse the chickpeas thoroughly, then pat them dry with a clean kitchen towel.
3. In a bowl, toss the chickpeas with olive oil, smoked paprika, ground cumin, garlic powder, salt, and black pepper until evenly coated.
4. Spread the chickpeas in a single layer on the prepared baking tray.
5. Roast in the preheated oven for 25-30 minutes, shaking the tray halfway through cooking, until the chickpeas are golden brown and crispy.
6. Remove from the oven and let cool slightly before serving.

Serving Suggestions:
Serve alongside a bowl of low-fat yoghurt mixed with lemon juice and fresh herbs like parsley or dill for dipping.

Nutritional Information (Per Serving):
Calories: 180 kcal | Total Fat: 7 g (Saturated Fat: 1 g) | Cholesterol: 0 mg | Fibre: 6 g | Protein: 8 g

Stuffed Avocado with Black Beans

Preparation Time: 5 minutes | **Servings:** 1

Ingredients:
1 ripe avocado, halved and pitted
1/4 cup canned black beans, drained and rinsed
1 tbsp fresh lime juice
1 tbsp fresh coriander, chopped
1/4 tsp ground cumin
Salt and pepper, to taste
A few cherry tomatoes, chopped (optional)

Instructions:
1. Cut the avocado in half and remove the pit.
2. Scoop out a little of the flesh from each half and place it in a small bowl.
3. Mash the avocado flesh and mix it with the black beans, lime juice, coriander, cumin, salt, and pepper.
4. Spoon the mixture back into the avocado halves.
5. Garnish with chopped cherry tomatoes (optional) and serve immediately.

Serving Suggestions:
Serve with a side of wholemeal crackers or vegetable sticks.

Nutritional Information (Per Serving):
Calories: 300 kcal | Total Fat: 18 g (Saturated Fat: 2.5 g) | Cholesterol: 0 mg | Fibre: 9 g | Protein: 6 g

Roasted Red Pepper and Almond Dip

Preparation Time: 10 minutes | **Cooking Time:** 20 minutes | **Servings:** 1

Ingredients:
1 red bell pepper, halved and deseeded
1/4 cup almonds (or almond butter)
1 tbsp olive oil
1 tsp lemon juice
1/4 tsp smoked paprika
Salt and pepper, to taste
A small handful of fresh parsley (optional)

Instructions:
1. Preheat the oven to 200°C (180°C fan) or 400°F. Place the red pepper halves on a baking tray, skin side up, and roast for 20 minutes, or until the skin is charred.
2. Once roasted, remove the pepper from the oven, allow it to cool slightly, then peel off the skin.
3. In a blender or food processor, combine the roasted pepper, almonds (or almond butter), olive oil, lemon juice, smoked paprika, salt, and pepper. Blend until smooth.
4. Transfer the dip to a bowl and refrigerate for at least 30 minutes before serving.
5. Garnish with chopped parsley if desired.

Serving Suggestions:
Serve with vegetable sticks (carrot, celery, cucumber) or wholemeal pita bread.

Nutritional Information (Per Serving):
Calories: 180 kcal | Total Fat: 14 g (Saturated Fat: 1 g) | Cholesterol: 0 mg | Fibre: 4 g | Protein: 5 g

Desserts

Sweet Treats for a Low Cholesterol Lifestyle

Desserts can feel like the ultimate indulgence, but in this low-cholesterol cookbook, they're reimagined to be lighter, healthier, and just as delicious. Packed with natural sweetness, nutrient-rich ingredients, and alternatives to traditional high-cholesterol ingredients, these recipes ensure you can enjoy dessert without compromise.

Why Desserts Fit into a Low Cholesterol Diet

Desserts don't have to be off-limits when managing cholesterol. This collection of recipes focuses on heart-healthy ingredients that support your goals while delivering satisfying flavours. Whether you're enjoying a fruity sorbet, a soft banana loaf, or a classic crumble, these recipes show that sweet treats can be both delicious and wholesome.

Key features of these desserts:
- **Low in Saturated Fat**: Ingredients like olive oil, coconut oil, almond milk, and plant-based yoghurt replace butter and cream to keep these recipes cholesterol-friendly.
- **Rich in Fibre**: Many of these recipes incorporate fruits, oats, nuts, and wholemeal flour, which support heart health and digestion.
- **Naturally Sweetened**: Using honey, maple syrup, and fruit as sweeteners helps reduce reliance on refined sugar.

Tips for Enjoying Desserts While Managing Cholesterol
1. **Prioritise Ingredients**: Look for recipes with whole grains, fresh fruit, and healthy fats like nuts and seeds.
2. **Portion Wisely**: Enjoying desserts in moderate portions helps keep your meals balanced and satisfying.
3. **Get Creative with Substitutions**: Experiment with plant-based milk, apple sauce, and nut butters to replace dairy or saturated fat-heavy ingredients.
4. **Add Freshness**: Pair desserts with fresh fruit or herbs for an extra layer of flavour and nutrition.

A Note on British Flavours

This chapter stays true to British favourites while embracing modern, health-conscious tweaks. From Victoria sponge cake made with ground almonds and apple sauce to a warm and comforting apple crumble, these desserts celebrate tradition with a lighter twist.

Let these recipes prove that desserts can be both indulgent and nourishing, fitting perfectly into your low cholesterol lifestyle.

Banana and Date Loaf

Preparation Time: 10 minutes | **Cooking Time:** 40-45 minutes | **Servings:** 1 loaf

Ingredients:

2 ripe bananas, mashed
100 g pitted dates, finely chopped
150 g wholemeal flour
1 teaspoon baking powder
1 teaspoon ground cinnamon
50 g unsweetened apple sauce
2 tablespoons olive oil
1 tablespoon honey (optional)
1 teaspoon vanilla extract
A pinch of salt

Instructions:

1. Preheat the oven to 180°C (160°C fan) or gas mark 4. Grease and line a loaf tin with parchment paper.
2. In a large bowl, combine the mashed bananas, chopped dates, apple sauce, olive oil, honey (if using), and vanilla extract.
3. In a separate bowl, mix the wholemeal flour, baking powder, ground cinnamon, and salt.
4. Gradually add the dry ingredients to the banana mixture, stirring gently until just combined.
5. Pour the batter into the prepared loaf tin and spread it evenly.
6. Bake in the preheated oven for 45-50 minutes, or until a skewer inserted into the centre comes out clean.
7. Allow the loaf to cool in the tin for 10 minutes before transferring to a wire rack to cool completely.

Serving Suggestions:

Pair with a dollop of low-fat plain yoghurt or a plant-based alternative for a balanced snack.

Nutritional Information (Per Serving):

Calories: 180 kcal | Total Fat: 5 g (Saturated Fat: 0.6 g) | Cholesterol: 0 mg | Fibre: 4 g | Protein: 3 g

Spiced Poached Pears with a Hint of Ginger

Preparation Time: 10 minutes | **Cooking Time:** 30 minutes | **Servings:** 1

Ingredients:

1 ripe but firm pear, peeled
200 ml water
1 teaspoon honey
1 small piece of cinnamon stick
¼ teaspoon ground ginger
1 clove
1 small strip of lemon peel
¼ teaspoon vanilla extract

Instructions:

1. In a small saucepan, combine the water, honey, cinnamon stick, ground ginger, clove, lemon peel, and vanilla extract. Bring the mixture to a simmer over medium heat.
2. Once simmering, carefully add the peeled pear to the spiced liquid, ensuring it is fully submerged.
3. Reduce the heat to low and simmer the pear for 20-25 minutes, turning it occasionally to ensure even cooking, until tender but still holding its shape.
4. Remove the pear from the liquid and set aside. Increase the heat under the liquid and simmer for an additional 5-10 minutes until it reduces and thickens slightly.
5. Drizzle the reduced spiced syrup over the poached pear before serving.

Serving Suggestions:

Sprinkle a handful of toasted almonds, hazelnuts, or pecans on top for added crunch and nutty flavour.

Nutritional Information (Per Serving):

Calories: 120 kcal | Total Fat: 0 g (Saturated Fat: 0 g) | Cholesterol: 0 mg | Fibre: 4 g | Protein: 1 g

Strawberry and Basil Sorbet

Preparation Time: 10 minutes | **Freezing Time:** 4 hours | **Servings:** 1

Ingredients:
150 g fresh strawberries, hulled
1 tablespoon honey or maple syrup
3-4 fresh basil leaves
1 tablespoon fresh lemon juice
50 ml water

Instructions:
1. In a blender, combine the strawberries, honey (or maple syrup), basil leaves, lemon juice, and water. Blend until the mixture is smooth.
2. Pour the mixture into a shallow container and place it in the freezer.
3. After 1 hour, stir the mixture to break up any ice crystals that form. Repeat this process every hour for 4 hours, or until the sorbet is fully frozen and smooth.
4. Scoop the sorbet into a bowl and serve immediately, garnished with a few fresh basil leaves if desired.

Serving Suggestions:
Accompany the sorbet with a small bowl of mixed fresh berries like blueberries, raspberries, or blackberries for added texture and sweetness.

Nutritional Information (Per Serving):
Calories: 90 kcal | Total Fat: 10 g (Saturated Fat: 0 g) | Cholesterol: 0 mg | Fibre: 3 g | Protein: 1 g

Vanilla Rice Pudding with Berry Compote

Preparation Time: 5 minutes | **Cooking Time:** 30 minutes | **Servings:** 1

Ingredients:
50 g pudding rice
250 ml unsweetened almond milk
(or other plant-based milk)
1 teaspoon vanilla extract
1 tablespoon honey or maple syrup
(optional)
A pinch of salt
50 g mixed berries (fresh or frozen)
1 teaspoon honey or maple syrup
1 teaspoon lemon juice

Instructions:
1. In a medium saucepan, combine the pudding rice, almond milk, vanilla extract, honey (if using), and a pinch of salt.
2. Bring the mixture to a simmer over medium heat, stirring occasionally to prevent sticking.
3. Reduce the heat to low and cook for 25-30 minutes, stirring frequently, until the rice is tender, and the mixture is creamy.
4. While the rice pudding is cooking, prepare the berry compote. In a small saucepan, combine the berries, honey, and lemon juice. Simmer over medium heat for 5-7 minutes, until the berries are softened, and the mixture has thickened slightly.
5. Once the rice pudding is ready, remove it from the heat and let it cool slightly.
6. Serve the rice pudding warm or chilled, topped with the berry compote.

Serving Suggestions:
Serve alongside a wholemeal biscuit or oatcake for a satisfying textural contrast.

Nutritional Information (Per Serving):
Calories: 200 kcal | Total Fat: 2 g (Saturated Fat: 0 g) | Cholesterol: 0 mg | Fibre: 4 g | Protein: 5 g

Apricot and Pistachio Energy Bites

Preparation Time: 10 minutes | **Cooking Time:** 30 minutes | **Servings:** 1

Ingredients:
50 g dried apricots, finely chopped
30 g unsalted pistachios, roughly chopped
20 g oats
1 tablespoon almond butter
1 tablespoon honey or maple syrup
1 teaspoon chia seeds
A pinch of salt

Instructions:
1. In a bowl, combine the chopped apricots, pistachios, oats, almond butter, honey (or maple syrup), chia seeds, and a pinch of salt. Mix well until all the ingredients are evenly incorporated.
2. Using your hands, form the mixture into small balls (about 2.5 cm in diameter).
3. Place the energy bites on a plate or tray and refrigerate for at least 30 minutes to firm up.
4. Once chilled, enjoy immediately or store in an airtight container in the fridge for up to a week.

Serving Suggestions:
For an indulgent twist, drizzle with a small amount of melted dark chocolate and let it set before chilling.

Nutritional Information (Per Serving):
Calories: 100 kcal | Total Fat: 4 g (Saturated Fat: 0.5 g) | Cholesterol: 0 mg | Fibre: 3 g | Protein: 3 g

Raspberry and Almond Yoghurt Pots

Preparation Time: 5 minutes | **Cooking Time:** 0 minutes | **Servings:** 1

Ingredients:
150 g plain unsweetened almond yoghurt
50 g fresh raspberries
1 tablespoon flaked almonds, toasted
1 teaspoon honey or maple syrup (optional)
1 teaspoon chia seeds

Instructions:
1. In a small serving pot or glass, spoon half of the almond yoghurt.
2. Layer half of the fresh raspberries on top of the yoghurt.
3. Add the remaining almond yoghurt on top of the raspberries.
4. Sprinkle the flaked almonds, chia seeds, and the remaining raspberries over the top.
5. Drizzle with honey or maple syrup if desired.
6. Serve immediately or refrigerate for up to 1 hour if you prefer it chilled.

Serving Suggestions:
Top with a tablespoon of wholegrain granola or crushed oat biscuits for added crunch.

Nutritional Information (Per Serving):
Calories: 140 kcal | Total Fat: 6 g (Saturated Fat: 0.5 g) | Cholesterol: 0 mg | Fibre: 4 g | Protein: 5 g

Low-Cholesterol Victoria Sponge Cake

Preparation Time: 15 minutes | **Cooking Time:** 20-25 minutes | **Servings:** 8 slices

Ingredients:
150 g self-raising flour
1 teaspoon baking powder
50 g ground almonds
100 g unsweetened apple sauce
3 tablespoons light olive oil
2 tablespoons honey or maple syrup
150 ml unsweetened almond milk
(or other plant-based milk)
1 teaspoon vanilla extract
A pinch of salt

For the Filling:
100 g fresh strawberries, sliced
2 tablespoons no-added-sugar
strawberry jam
100 g low-fat plain yoghurt (or
dairy-free alternative)

Instructions:
1. Preheat the oven to 180°C (160°C fan) or gas mark 4. Grease and line two 18 cm round cake tins with parchment paper.
2. In a large bowl, sift together the self-raising flour, baking powder, ground almonds, and a pinch of salt.
3. In a separate bowl, whisk together the apple sauce, olive oil, honey (or maple syrup), almond milk, and vanilla extract until smooth.
4. Gradually fold the wet ingredients into the dry ingredients, stirring gently until just combined.
5. Divide the batter evenly between the two prepared cake tins and spread it out smoothly.
6. Bake in the preheated oven for 20-25 minutes, or until a skewer inserted into the centre of the cakes comes out clean.
7. Allow the cakes to cool in the tins for 5 minutes, then transfer them to a wire rack to cool completely.
8. Once cooled, spread the jam and yoghurt over one of the cakes. Layer the sliced strawberries on top, then place the second cake on top to form a sandwich.
9. Dust lightly with icing sugar (optional) before serving.

Serving Suggestions:
Pair a slice of the sponge cake with a small scoop of fruit sorbet, such as lemon or raspberry, for a refreshing complement.

Nutritional Information (Per Serving):
Calories: 170 kcal | Total Fat: 7 g (Saturated Fat: 1 g) | Cholesterol: 0 mg | Fibre: 3 g | Protein: 4 g

Dark Chocolate and Orange Mousse

Preparation Time: 10 minutes | **Chilling Time:** 1 hour | **Servings:** 1

Ingredients:
30 g dark chocolate (70% cocoa or higher), melted
50 ml aquafaba (liquid from a can of chickpeas)
½ teaspoon orange zest
½ teaspoon vanilla extract
1 teaspoon honey or maple syrup (optional)
A pinch of salt

Instructions:
1. Melt the dark chocolate in a heatproof bowl over a pot of simmering water, or in the microwave in short bursts, stirring until smooth. Set aside to cool slightly.
2. In a clean bowl, whisk the aquafaba with a pinch of salt using an electric mixer until stiff peaks form, similar to egg whites. This may take 5-7 minutes.
3. Gently fold the melted chocolate into the whipped aquafaba, being careful not to deflate the mixture. Add the orange zest, vanilla extract, and honey or maple syrup if using, and fold until combined.
4. Spoon the mixture into a serving glass or small bowl.
5. Refrigerate for at least 1 hour, or until set and chilled.
6. Garnish with additional orange zest or a small piece of dark chocolate if desired, before serving.

Serving Suggestions:
Serve with a few fresh orange slices or segments on the side for added colour and a burst of citrus flavour.

Nutritional Information (Per Serving):
Calories: 120 kcal | Total Fat: 6 g (Saturated Fat: 3 g) | Cholesterol: 0 mg | Fibre: 3 g | Protein: 2 g

Honey and Oat Flapjacks

Preparation Time: 5 minutes | **Cooking Time:** 20-25 minutes | **Servings:** 8

Ingredients:
200 g rolled oats
100 g honey
50 g light olive oil or coconut oil
1 teaspoon vanilla extract
2 tablespoons ground flaxseeds
50 g dried fruit (e.g., sultanas, apricots)
A pinch of salt

Instructions:
1. Preheat the oven to 180°C (160°C fan) or gas mark 4. Line a square baking tin with parchment paper.
2. In a small saucepan, gently heat the honey and olive oil (or coconut oil) over low heat until melted and combined. Remove from heat and stir in the vanilla extract.
3. In a large bowl, mix the oats, ground flaxseeds, dried fruit, and a pinch of salt.
4. Pour the honey mixture over the oats and stir well until everything is coated evenly.
5. Press the mixture into the prepared baking tin, smoothing it out into an even layer.
6. Bake in the preheated oven for 20-25 minutes, or until golden brown.
7. Allow the flapjacks to cool in the tin for 10 minutes before transferring to a wire rack to cool completely. Once cool, cut into squares.

Serving Suggestions:
Sprinkle desiccated coconut over the flapjack mixture before baking for a tropical touch.

Nutritional Information (Per Serving):
Calories: 180 kcal | Total Fat: 6 g (Saturated Fat: 1 g) | Cholesterol: 0 mg | Fibre: 3 g | Protein: 3 g

Blueberry and Lemon Drizzle Traybake

Preparation Time: 10 minutes | **Cooking Time:** 25 minutes | **Servings:** 9 squares

Ingredients:
150 g wholemeal flour
50 g ground almonds
1 teaspoon baking powder
100 g unsweetened apple sauce
50 ml light olive oil
2 tablespoons honey or maple syrup
150 ml unsweetened almond milk (or other plant-based milk)
1 teaspoon vanilla extract
Zest of 1 lemon
100 g fresh blueberries
For the Lemon Drizzle:
Juice of 1 lemon
1 tablespoon honey or maple syrup

Instructions:
1. Preheat the oven to 180°C (160°C fan) or gas mark 4. Grease and line a square baking tin with parchment paper.
2. In a large bowl, sift together the wholemeal flour, ground almonds, and baking powder.
3. In a separate bowl, whisk together the apple sauce, olive oil, honey (or maple syrup), almond milk, vanilla extract, and lemon zest.
4. Gradually fold the wet ingredients into the dry ingredients, mixing gently until just combined.
5. Fold in the blueberries carefully, ensuring they are evenly distributed throughout the batter.
6. Pour the batter into the prepared baking tin and spread it out evenly.
7. Bake in the preheated oven for 25-30 minutes, or until a skewer inserted into the centre comes out clean.
8. While the traybake is cooling, prepare the lemon drizzle by mixing the lemon juice and honey (or maple syrup) together in a small bowl.
9. Once the traybake has cooled slightly, prick the top with a skewer and drizzle the lemon mixture evenly over the cake.
10. Allow the drizzle to soak in, then cut the traybake into squares before serving.

Serving Suggestions:
Sprinkle a few chopped almonds or pistachios on top.

Nutritional Information (Per Serving):
Calories: 150 kcal | Total Fat: 6 g (Saturated Fat: 1 g) | Cholesterol: 0 mg | Fibre: 3 g | Protein: 4 g

Baked Plums with Cinnamon and Maple Syrup

Preparation Time: 5 minutes | **Cooking Time:** 20 minutes | **Servings:** 1

Ingredients:
2 ripe plums, halved and pitted
1 teaspoon maple syrup
¼ teaspoon ground cinnamon
A small pinch of ground nutmeg
(optional)
1 teaspoon lemon juice
A few fresh mint leaves for garnish
(optional)

Instructions:
1. Preheat the oven to 180°C (160°C fan) or gas mark 4.
2. Place the halved and pitted plums in a small baking dish, cut side up.
3. Drizzle the maple syrup and lemon juice over the plums, then sprinkle with cinnamon and a pinch of nutmeg if using.
4. Bake in the preheated oven for 15-20 minutes, or until the plums are tender and lightly caramelised.
5. Remove from the oven and allow to cool slightly.
6. Serve warm, garnished with fresh mint leaves if desired.

Serving Suggestions:
Pair with a warm cup of mint tea for a light evening snack.

Nutritional Information (Per Serving):
Calories: 80 kcal | Total Fat: 0 g (Saturated Fat: 0 g) | Cholesterol: 0 mg | Fibre: 2 g | Protein: 1 g

Peach and Passionfruit Eton Mess

Preparation Time: 10 minutes | **Cooking Time:** 0 minutes | **Servings:** 1

Ingredients:
1 ripe peach, sliced
1 passionfruit, pulp scooped out
100 g low-fat plain yoghurt (or
dairy-free alternative)
1 tablespoon crushed meringue
(low-fat or vegan, if preferred)
1 teaspoon honey or maple syrup
(optional)
A few fresh mint leaves for garnish
(optional)

Instructions:
1. In a small serving bowl or glass, layer half of the yoghurt.
2. Add half of the sliced peach and passionfruit pulp on top of the yoghurt.
3. Add a layer of crushed meringue.
4. Repeat the layers with the remaining yoghurt, peach slices, and passionfruit.
5. Drizzle with honey or maple syrup if desired.
6. Garnish with fresh mint leaves, if using, and serve immediately.

Serving Suggestions:
Serve in a tall glass for a parfait-style presentation, showcasing the vibrant layers of fruit, yoghurt, and meringue.

Nutritional Information (Per Serving):
Calories: 120 kcal | Total Fat: 1 g (Saturated Fat: 0 g) | Cholesterol: 0 mg | Fibre: 3 g | Protein: 4 g

Apple and Cinnamon Oat Crumble

Preparation Time: 10 minutes | **Cooking Time:** 25-30 minutes | **Servings:** 1

Ingredients:
1 medium apple, peeled, cored, and chopped
1 teaspoon lemon juice
1 teaspoon ground cinnamon
1 tablespoon honey or maple syrup
30 g rolled oats
1 tablespoon wholemeal flour
1 tablespoon olive oil or coconut oil
A pinch of salt

Instructions:
1. Preheat the oven to 180°C (160°C fan) or gas mark 4.
2. In a small baking dish, toss the chopped apple with the lemon juice, ½ teaspoon of cinnamon, and half of the honey or maple syrup. Spread the mixture evenly across the dish.
3. In a separate bowl, combine the rolled oats, wholemeal flour, olive oil (or coconut oil), the remaining cinnamon, the rest of the honey or maple syrup, and a pinch of salt. Mix until the oats are evenly coated and crumbly.
4. Sprinkle the oat mixture evenly over the apples in the baking dish.
5. Bake in the preheated oven for 25-30 minutes, or until the topping is golden and the apples are tender.
6. Remove from the oven and allow to cool slightly before serving.

Serving Suggestions:
If serving to guests, a light drizzle of honey just before serving adds a final touch of sweetness and shine.

Nutritional Information (Per Serving):
Calories: 200 kcal | Total Fat: 6 g (Saturated Fat: 1 g) | Cholesterol: 0 mg | Fibre: 5 g | Protein: 3 g

Chilled Mango and Coconut Rice Pudding

Preparation Time: 10 minutes | **Cooking Time:** 25-30 minutes | **Chilling Time:** 1 hour | **Servings:** 1

Ingredients:
50 g pudding rice
200 ml light coconut milk
1 tablespoon honey or maple syrup
½ teaspoon vanilla extract
A pinch of salt
½ ripe mango, diced

Instructions:
1. In a saucepan, combine the pudding rice, coconut milk, honey (or maple syrup), vanilla extract, and a pinch of salt.
2. Bring the mixture to a simmer over medium heat, stirring occasionally.
3. Reduce the heat to low and cook for 25-30 minutes, stirring frequently, until the rice is tender and the mixture is creamy.
4. Remove the rice pudding from the heat and allow it to cool slightly.
5. Once cooled, refrigerate for at least 1 hour, or until chilled.
6. Before serving, top the chilled rice pudding with diced mango.
7. Optional: Garnish with a sprinkle of desiccated coconut or a few fresh mint leaves for extra flavour.

Serving Suggestions:
Pair with other tropical fruits like passionfruit, pineapple, or papaya for a vibrant plate.

Nutritional Information (Per Serving):
Calories: 200 kcal | Total Fat: 6 g (Saturated Fat: 4 g) | Cholesterol: 0 mg | Fibre: 3 g | Protein: 3 g

Avocado and Lime Mousse

Preparation Time: 10 minutes | **Chilling Time:** 2 hours | **Servings:** 1

Ingredients:
1 ripe avocado, peeled and pitted
1/2 cup low-fat coconut milk
2 tbsp maple syrup or agave syrup
Zest and juice of 1 lime
1/4 tsp vanilla extract
Fresh mint leaves (for garnish)

Instructions:
1. In a blender or food processor, combine the avocado, coconut milk, maple syrup, lime zest, lime juice, and vanilla extract.
2. Blend until smooth and creamy, scraping down the sides as needed.
3. Taste and adjust sweetness or lime juice if desired.
4. Transfer the mousse to a serving dish and refrigerate for at least 2 hours to set.
5. Garnish with fresh mint leaves before serving.

Serving Suggestions:
Serve with a sprinkle of toasted coconut or a few crushed almonds for added texture.

Nutritional Information (Per Serving):
Calories: 250 kcal | Total Fat: 18 g (Saturated Fat: 3 g) | Cholesterol: 0 mg | Fibre: 8 g | Protein: 3 g

Pumpkin and Ginger Pudding

Preparation Time: 10 minutes | **Cooking Time:** 30 minutes | **Servings:** 1

Ingredients:
120 g pumpkin purée (fresh or canned, without added sugar)
60 ml unsweetened almond milk (or other plant-based milk)
1 tbsp ground ginger
1/2 tsp ground cinnamon
1 tbsp maple syrup or agave syrup
1/2 tsp vanilla extract

Instructions:
1. In a saucepan, combine the pumpkin purée, almond milk, ground ginger, cinnamon, maple syrup, and vanilla extract.
2. Heat over medium heat, stirring occasionally, until the mixture is warm and smooth (about 5 minutes).
3. Reduce the heat and continue to cook for 20–25 minutes, stirring frequently, until the pudding thickens.
4. Pour the mixture into a small bowl or individual serving dishes and leave to cool.
5. Refrigerate for 1–2 hours before serving.

Serving Suggestions:
Pair with a fresh fruit salad or a light oat biscuit for added crunch.

Nutritional Information (Per Serving):
Calories: 180 kcal | Total Fat: 3 g (Saturated Fat: 0 g) | Cholesterol: 0 mg | Fibre: 6 g | Protein: 2 g

Smoothies

Smoothies are a wonderful way to enjoy nutritious, heart-friendly ingredients in a convenient and delicious form. Whether you're craving a tropical immune booster, a creamy avocado treat, or a revitalising berry blend, these recipes are designed to fit seamlessly into your low-cholesterol lifestyle.

Why Smoothies Work in a Low-Cholesterol Diet

Smoothies aren't just refreshing; they're packed with essential nutrients that support heart health while keeping cholesterol levels in check. These recipes are crafted with fibre-rich fruits, vegetables, and superfoods to help maintain healthy cholesterol levels and provide long-lasting energy.

Key Features of These Smoothies

- **Low in Saturated Fats**: Bases like almond milk, coconut water, and whole fruits keep these recipes light and cholesterol-free.
- **Rich in Fibre**: Ingredients such as oats, chia seeds, and leafy greens provide fibre to support cholesterol management.
- **Full of Antioxidants**: Superfoods like berries, turmeric, and ginger bring powerful anti-inflammatory benefits to every sip.

Tips for Making the Perfect Smoothie

- **Choose the Right Base**: Opt for unsweetened plant-based milk or coconut water for a light, heart-healthy foundation.
- **Add Texture**: Include oats, chia seeds, or flaxseeds for added fibre and creaminess.
- **Balance Flavours**: Use naturally sweet fruits like bananas and dates to counter tart or earthy ingredients like kale or turmeric.
- **Enhance Absorption**: Add a pinch of black pepper when using turmeric to maximise its benefits.
- **Experiment with Herbs**: Fresh mint, basil, or coriander can give your smoothie an extra layer of refreshing flavour.

Enjoy these vibrant and nourishing drinks as part of your low-cholesterol journey—they're quick, delicious, and packed with benefits.

Pineapple and Turmeric Anti-Inflammatory Smoothie

Preparation Time: 5 minutes | **Servings:** 1

Ingredients:
100 g fresh pineapple chunks
1 small banana
1 teaspoon ground turmeric
½ teaspoon ground ginger or a
small piece of fresh ginger
150 ml coconut water
1 teaspoon chia seeds
Juice of ½ lemon
A pinch of black pepper (to enhance
turmeric absorption)
Ice cubes (optional)

Instructions:
1. Add all the ingredients—pineapple, banana, turmeric, ginger, coconut water, chia seeds, lemon juice, and black pepper—into a blender.
2. Blend until smooth and creamy.
3. If desired, add ice cubes and blend again to chill the smoothie.
4. Pour into a glass and serve immediately.

Nutritional Information (Per Serving):
Calories: 140 kcal | Total Fat: 2 g (Saturated Fat: 0.5 g) | Cholesterol: 0 mg | Fibre: 4 g | Protein: 2 g

Beetroot and Berry Antioxidant Shake

Preparation Time: 5 minutes   **Servings:** 1

Ingredients:
1 small cooked beetroot, peeled and
chopped
100 g mixed berries (e.g.,
blueberries, raspberries,
strawberries)
1 small banana
150 ml unsweetened almond milk
(or other plant-based milk)
1 tablespoon chia seeds
1 teaspoon honey or maple syrup
(optional)
Ice cubes (optional)

Instructions:
1. Add the beetroot, mixed berries, banana, almond milk, chia seeds, and honey (if using) into a blender.
2. Blend until smooth and creamy.
3. Add ice cubes if you prefer a chilled shake, and blend again.
4. Pour into a glass and serve immediately.

Nutritional Information (Per Serving):
Calories: 160 kcal | Total Fat: 3 g (Saturated Fat: 0 g) | Cholesterol: 0 mg | Fibre: 6 g | Protein: 4 g

Cherry and Almond Energy Smoothie

Preparation Time: 5 minutes | **Servings:** 1

Ingredients:
100 g fresh or frozen cherries, pitted
1 tablespoon almond butter
1 small banana
150 ml unsweetened almond milk
1 tablespoon oats
1 teaspoon honey or maple syrup
(optional)
Ice cubes (optional)

Instructions:
1. Add the cherries, almond butter, banana, almond milk, oats, and honey (if using) into a blender.
2. Blend until smooth and creamy.
3. If you prefer a chilled smoothie, add a few ice cubes and blend again.
4. Pour into a glass and serve immediately.

Nutritional Information (Per Serving):
Calories: 220 kcal | Total Fat: 9 g (Saturated Fat: 1 g) | Cholesterol: 0 mg | Fibre: 5 g | Protein: 6 g

Green Goodness Kiwi and Spinach Smoothie

Preparation Time: 5 minutes | **Servings:** 1

Ingredients:
1 ripe kiwi, peeled and chopped
A handful of fresh spinach
1 small banana
150 ml unsweetened almond milk
(or other plant-based milk)
1 teaspoon chia seeds
Juice of ½ lime
1 teaspoon honey or maple syrup
(optional)
Ice cubes (optional)

Instructions:
1. Add the kiwi, spinach, banana, almond milk, chia seeds, lime juice, and honey (if using) into a blender.
2. Blend until smooth and creamy.
3. If desired, add ice cubes and blend again for a chilled smoothie.
4. Pour into a glass and serve immediately.

Nutritional Information (Per Serving):
Calories: 130 kcal | Total Fat: 2 g (Saturated Fat: 0 g) | Cholesterol: 0 mg | Fibre: 5 g | Protein: 3 g

Creamy Avocado and Lime Smoothie

Preparation Time: 5 minutes | **Servings:** 1

Ingredients:
½ ripe avocado
1 small banana
Juice of 1 lime
150 ml unsweetened almond milk
(or other plant-based milk)
1 teaspoon honey or maple syrup
(optional)
1 tablespoon chia seeds
Ice cubes (optional)

Instructions:
1. Scoop the avocado into a blender and add the banana, lime juice, almond milk, honey (if using), and chia seeds.
2. Blend until smooth and creamy.
3. If you prefer a chilled smoothie, add a few ice cubes and blend again.
4. Pour into a glass and serve immediately.

Nutritional Information (Per Serving):
Calories: 200 kcal | Total Fat: 11 g (Saturated Fat: 1.5 g) | Cholesterol: 0 mg | Fibre: 7 g | Protein: 4 g

Strawberry and Basil Detox Blend

Preparation Time: 5 minutes | **Servings:** 1

Ingredients:
100 g fresh strawberries, hulled
A handful of fresh basil leaves
1 small cucumber, chopped
150 ml coconut water
Juice of ½ lemon
1 teaspoon chia seeds
Ice cubes (optional)

Instructions:
1. Add the strawberries, basil leaves, cucumber, coconut water, lemon juice, and chia seeds into a blender.
2. Blend until smooth and well combined.
3. If you prefer a chilled drink, add ice cubes and blend again.
4. Pour into a glass and serve immediately.

Nutritional Information (Per Serving):
Calories: 80 kcal | Total Fat: 1 g (Saturated Fat: 0 g) | Cholesterol: 0 mg | Fibre: 4 g | Protein: 2 g

Blueberry and Flaxseed Power Shake

Preparation Time: 5 minutes | **Servings:** 1

Ingredients:
100 g fresh or frozen blueberries
1 small banana
1 tablespoon ground flaxseeds
150 ml unsweetened almond milk
(or other plant-based milk)
1 teaspoon honey or maple syrup
(optional)
1 tablespoon oats
Ice cubes (optional)

Instructions:
1. Add the blueberries, banana, ground flaxseeds, almond milk, honey (if using), and oats into a blender.
2. Blend until smooth and creamy.
3. If desired, add ice cubes and blend again for a chilled shake.
4. Pour into a glass and serve immediately.

Nutritional Information (Per Serving):
Calories: 180 kcal | Total Fat: 5 g (Saturated Fat: 0.5 g) | Cholesterol: 0 mg | Fibre: 6 g | Protein: 4 g

Banana, Date, and Cinnamon Smoothie

Preparation Time: 5 minutes | **Servings:** 1

Ingredients:
1 small banana
2 pitted dates
150 ml unsweetened almond milk
(or other plant-based milk)
½ teaspoon ground cinnamon
1 teaspoon chia seeds
1 teaspoon honey or maple syrup
(optional)
Ice cubes (optional)

Instructions:
1. Add the banana, dates, almond milk, cinnamon, chia seeds, and honey (if using) into a blender.
2. Blend until smooth and creamy.
3. Add ice cubes if you prefer a chilled smoothie, and blend again.
4. Pour into a glass and serve immediately.

Nutritional Information (Per Serving):
Calories: 180 kcal | Total Fat: 3 g (Saturated Fat: 0.5 g) | Cholesterol: 0 mg | Fibre: 5 g | Protein: 3 g

Cucumber, Celery, and Apple Cleanse Smoothie

Preparation Time: 5 minutes | **Servings:** 1

Ingredients:
½ cucumber, chopped
1 celery stalk, chopped
1 small apple, cored and chopped
Juice of ½ lemon
150 ml coconut water
A handful of fresh spinach
(optional)
Ice cubes (optional)

Instructions:
1. Add the cucumber, celery, apple, lemon juice, coconut water, and spinach (if using) into a blender.
2. Blend until smooth and well combined.
3. Add ice cubes if you prefer a chilled smoothie, and blend again.
4. Pour into a glass and serve immediately.

Nutritional Information (Per Serving):
Calories: 90 kcal | Total Fat: 0 g (Saturated Fat: 0 g) | Cholesterol: 0 mg | Fibre: 4 g | Protein: 2 g

Berry and Oat Breakfast Smoothie

Preparation Time: 5 minutes | **Servings:** 1

Ingredients:
100 g mixed berries (fresh or frozen)
1 small banana
2 tablespoons rolled oats
150 ml unsweetened almond milk (or other plant-based milk)
1 tablespoon chia seeds
1 teaspoon honey or maple syrup (optional)
Ice cubes (optional)

Instructions:
1. Add the mixed berries, banana, rolled oats, almond milk, chia seeds, and honey (if using) into a blender.
2. Blend until smooth and creamy.
3. Add ice cubes if you prefer a chilled smoothie, and blend again.
4. Pour into a glass and serve immediately.

Nutritional Information (Per Serving):
Calories: 190 kcal | Total Fat: 4 g (Saturated Fat: 0.5 g) | Cholesterol: 0 mg | Fibre: 6 g | Protein: 4 g

Peach and Chia Seed Hydration Smoothie

Preparation Time: 5 minutes | **Servings:** 1

Ingredients:
1 ripe peach, sliced (fresh or frozen)
1 teaspoon chia seeds
150 ml coconut water
1 small banana
Juice of ½ lime
Ice cubes (optional)

Instructions:
1. Add the peach slices, chia seeds, coconut water, banana, and lime juice into a blender.
2. Blend until smooth and well combined.
3. Add ice cubes if you prefer a chilled smoothie, and blend again.
4. Pour into a glass and serve immediately.

Nutritional Information (Per Serving):
Calories: 120 kcal | Total Fat: 2 g (Saturated Fat: 0 g) | Cholesterol: 0 mg | Fibre: 4 g | Protein: 2 g

Pineapple and Kale Immune Booster

Preparation Time: 5 minutes | **Servings:** 1

Ingredients:
100 g fresh pineapple chunks
A handful of fresh kale leaves, stems removed
1 small banana
150 ml coconut water
½ teaspoon grated fresh ginger
Juice of ½ lemon
Ice cubes (optional)

Instructions:
1. Add the pineapple, kale, banana, coconut water, ginger, and lemon juice into a blender.
2. Blend until smooth and creamy.
3. Add ice cubes if you prefer a chilled smoothie, and blend again.
4. Pour into a glass and serve immediately.

Nutritional Information (Per Serving):
Calories: 110 kcal | Total Fat: 1 g (Saturated Fat: 0 g) | Cholesterol: 0 mg | Fibre: 4 g | Protein: 3 g

Carrot and Orange Vitamin Boost Smoothie

Preparation Time: 10 minutes | **Servings:** 1

Ingredients:

1 medium carrot, peeled and chopped
Juice of 1 orange
1 small banana
100 ml coconut water (or cold water)
½ teaspoon grated fresh ginger (optional)
1 teaspoon chia seeds
Ice cubes (optional)

Instructions:

1. Add the chopped carrot, orange juice, banana, coconut water, ginger (if using), and chia seeds into a blender.
2. Blend until smooth and well combined.
3. If you prefer a chilled smoothie, add ice cubes and blend again.
4. Pour into a glass and serve immediately.

Nutritional Information (Per Serving):

Calories: 120 kcal | Total Fat: 1 g (Saturated Fat: 0 g) | Cholesterol: 0 mg | Fibre: 5 g | Protein: 2 g

Cucumber and Mint Refresher

Preparation Time: 5 minutes | **Servings:** 1

Ingredients:

½ cucumber, chopped
A handful of fresh mint leaves
Juice of ½ lime
150 ml coconut water (or cold water)
1 teaspoon honey or maple syrup (optional)
Ice cubes (optional)

Instructions:

1. Add the chopped cucumber, mint leaves, lime juice, coconut water, and honey (if using) into a blender.
2. Blend until smooth and well combined.
3. If desired, add ice cubes and blend again for a chilled refresher.
4. Pour into a glass and serve immediately.

Nutritional Information (Per Serving):

Calories: 50 kcal | Total Fat: 0 g (Saturated Fat: 0 g) | Cholesterol: 0 mg | Fibre: 1 g | Protein: 1 g

Bonus Chapter 1: Sauces and Dressings

Elevate your meals with this collection of heart-healthy sauces and dressings. These recipes are designed to complement your low-cholesterol lifestyle while adding flavour and variety to every dish. From zesty vinaigrettes to creamy dips and versatile salsas, this bonus chapter has something for everyone.

Why Sauces and Dressings Matter
A well-crafted sauce or dressing can transform a simple meal into a flavourful delight. These recipes are:
- **Low in Saturated Fats**: Using healthy fats like olive oil and tahini, they enhance taste without compromising your cholesterol goals.
- **Nutrient-Dense**: Packed with fresh herbs, citrus, and spices, these recipes deliver more than just flavour—they're rich in antioxidants and essential nutrients.
- **Quick and Easy**: Most recipes can be whipped up in minutes, making them perfect for busy lifestyles.

How to Use These Recipes
- **Dress Up Salads**: Pair vinaigrettes and creamy dressings with fresh greens and vegetables for a quick and satisfying salad.
- **Enhance Mains**: Use dips and sauces as accompaniments for roasted vegetables, grilled meats, or wholegrain breads.
- **Snack Smarter**: Pair these sauces with veggie sticks, crackers, or wholemeal pitta for a wholesome snack.

Get ready to add a burst of flavour to your meals with these nourishing, low-cholesterol creations!

Zesty Lemon and Herb Vinaigrette

Preparation Time: 5 minutes | **Servings:** 1

Ingredients:
Juice of 1 lemon
2 tablespoons olive oil
1 teaspoon Dijon mustard
1 tablespoon fresh parsley, chopped
1 tablespoon fresh basil, chopped
1 garlic clove, minced
½ teaspoon honey or maple syrup
(optional)
Salt and black pepper to taste

Instructions:
1. In a small bowl, whisk together the lemon juice, olive oil, Dijon mustard, garlic, and honey (if using).
2. Stir in the chopped parsley and basil.
3. Season with salt and black pepper to taste.
4. Serve immediately or store in an airtight container in the fridge for up to 3 days. Shake well before use.

Nutritional Information (Per Serving):
Calories: 90 kcal | Total Fat: 9 g (Saturated Fat: 1 g) | Cholesterol: 0 mg | Fibre: 41 g | Protein: 0 g

Smoky Aubergine and Garlic Dip

Preparation Time: 10 minutes | **Cooking Time:** 30-40 minutes | **Servings:** 1small bowl

Ingredients:
1 medium aubergine
2 garlic cloves, minced
1 tablespoon tahini
1 tablespoon lemon juice
1 teaspoon smoked paprika
1 tablespoon olive oil
Salt and black pepper to taste
Fresh parsley, chopped (for garnish)

Instructions:
1. Preheat the oven to 200°C (180°C fan) or gas mark 6.
2. Prick the aubergine with a fork and roast it in the oven for 30-40 minutes, turning occasionally, until the skin is charred and the flesh is soft.
3. Once cooked, remove the aubergine from the oven and let it cool slightly.
4. Peel the skin off the aubergine and scoop the flesh into a bowl.
5. Add the minced garlic, tahini, lemon juice, smoked paprika, and olive oil to the aubergine.
6. Mash or blend the mixture until smooth and well combined.
7. Season with salt and black pepper to taste.
8. Garnish with fresh parsley and serve with vegetables or wholemeal pita bread.

Nutritional Information (Per Serving):
Calories: 120 kcal | Total Fat: 6 g (Saturated Fat: 1 g) | Cholesterol: 0 mg | Fibre: 4 g | Protein: 3 g

Honey Mustard Yogurt Dressing

Preparation Time: 5 minutes | **Servings:** 1 small jar

Ingredients:
100 g low-fat plain yoghurt (or dairy-free alternative)
1 tablespoon Dijon mustard
1 tablespoon honey
1 teaspoon apple cider vinegar
1 tablespoon lemon juice
Salt and black pepper to taste

Instructions:
1. In a small bowl, whisk together the yoghurt, Dijon mustard, honey, apple cider vinegar, and lemon juice until smooth and well combined.
2. Season with salt and black pepper to taste.
3. Serve immediately or store in an airtight container in the fridge for up to 3 days. Shake or stir well before use.

Nutritional Information (Per Serving):
Calories: 50 kcal | Total Fat: 1 g (Saturated Fat: 0.5 g) | Cholesterol: 0 mg | Fibre: 0 g | Protein: 3 g

Spiced Tomato and Coriander Salsa

Preparation Time: 10 minutes || **Servings:** 1 small bowl

Ingredients:
4 medium ripe tomatoes, finely chopped
1 small red onion, finely chopped
1 garlic clove, minced
1 small red chilli, deseeded and finely chopped
1 tablespoon fresh coriander, chopped
Juice of 1 lime
½ teaspoon ground cumin
½ teaspoon smoked paprika
Salt and black pepper to taste

Instructions:
1. In a bowl, combine the chopped tomatoes, red onion, garlic, chilli, and coriander.
2. Add the lime juice, ground cumin, and smoked paprika.
3. Stir everything together until well mixed.
4. Season with salt and black pepper to taste.
5. Serve immediately or refrigerate for up to 2 days. Stir well before serving.

Nutritional Information (Per Serving):
Calories: 40 kcal | Total Fat: 0 g (Saturated Fat: 0 g) | Cholesterol: 0 mg | Fibre: 2 g | Protein: 1 g

Sweet Chilli and Lime Dipping Sauce

Preparation Time: 5 minutes | **Cooking Time:** 10 minutes | **Servings:** 1 small jar

Ingredients:
1 red chilli, finely chopped (deseeded for less heat)
2 tablespoons honey
2 tablespoons rice vinegar
1 tablespoon lime juice
1 garlic clove, minced
100 ml water
1 teaspoon cornflour (mixed with 1 tablespoon cold water to make a slurry)

Instructions:
1. In a small saucepan, combine the chopped chilli, honey, rice vinegar, lime juice, garlic, and water.
2. Bring the mixture to a simmer over medium heat and cook for 5-7 minutes, until the sauce begins to thicken.
3. Stir in the cornflour slurry and cook for another 2 minutes, or until the sauce has thickened to your desired consistency.
4. Remove from the heat and let it cool.
5. Serve immediately or store in an airtight container in the fridge for up to a week.

Nutritional Information (Per Serving):
Calories: 50 kcal | Total Fat: 0 g (Saturated Fat: 0 g) | Cholesterol: 0 mg | Fibre: 0 g | Protein: 0 g

Spicy Mango and Coriander Sauce

Preparation Time: 10 minutes | **Cooking Time:** 25 minutes | **Servings:** 1 small bowl

Ingredients:
1 ripe mango, peeled and chopped
1 small red chilli, deseeded and finely chopped
1 tablespoon fresh coriander, chopped
Juice of 1 lime
1 teaspoon honey (optional)
½ teaspoon ground cumin
Salt and black pepper to taste

Instructions:
1. In a blender, combine the chopped mango, red chilli, coriander, lime juice, honey (if using), and ground cumin.
2. Blend until smooth and creamy.
3. Season with salt and black pepper to taste.
4. Serve immediately or refrigerate for up to 3 days. Stir well before serving.

Nutritional Information (Per Serving):
Calories: 60 kcal | Total Fat: 0 g (Saturated Fat: 0 g) | Cholesterol: 0 mg | Fibre: 2 g | Protein: 1 g

Herby Lemon and Garlic Dressing

Preparation Time: 5 minutes | **Servings:** 1 small jar

Ingredients:
Juice of 1 lemon
2 tablespoons olive oil
1 garlic clove, minced
1 tablespoon fresh parsley, chopped
1 tablespoon fresh dill, chopped
1 teaspoon Dijon mustard
Salt and black pepper to taste

Instructions:
1. In a small bowl, whisk together the lemon juice, olive oil, garlic, Dijon mustard, parsley, and dill until well combined.
2. Season with salt and black pepper to taste.
3. Serve immediately or store in an airtight container in the fridge for up to 3 days. Shake or stir well before use.

Nutritional Information (Per Serving):
Calories: 80 kcal | Total Fat: 8 g (Saturated Fat: 1 g) | Cholesterol: 0 mg | Fibre: 1 g | Protein: 0 g

Garlic and Basil Pesto (Dairy-Free)

Preparation Time: 10 minutes | **Servings:** 1 small jar

Ingredients:
50 g fresh basil leaves
2 garlic cloves
30 g pine nuts (or sunflower seeds for a more affordable option)
3 tablespoons olive oil
1 tablespoon lemon juice
1 tablespoon nutritional yeast (optional, for a cheesy flavour)
Salt and black pepper to taste

Instructions:
1. In a food processor, combine the basil leaves, garlic, pine nuts (or sunflower seeds), lemon juice, and nutritional yeast (if using).
2. Blend while gradually adding the olive oil until the mixture reaches a smooth, pesto-like consistency.
3. Season with salt and black pepper to taste.
4. Serve immediately or store in an airtight container in the fridge for up to 5 days.

Nutritional Information (Per Serving):
Calories: 90 kcal | Total Fat: 8 g (Saturated Fat: 1 g) | Cholesterol: 0 mg | Fibre: 1 g | Protein: 2 g

Smoky Carrot and Cumin Dip

Preparation Time: 10 minutes | **Cooking Time:** 20 minutes | **Servings:** 1small bowl

Ingredients:
3 medium carrots, peeled and chopped
1 tablespoon olive oil
1 teaspoon ground cumin
½ teaspoon smoked paprika
1 garlic clove, minced
1 tablespoon lemon juice
1 tablespoon tahini
Salt and black pepper to taste
Fresh parsley for garnish (optional)

Instructions:
1. Preheat the oven to 200°C (180°C fan) or gas mark 6.
2. Toss the chopped carrots with olive oil, cumin, and smoked paprika. Spread them out on a baking tray and roast in the oven for 20 minutes or until soft and slightly caramelised.
3. Once roasted, transfer the carrots to a food processor. Add the minced garlic, lemon juice, tahini, and a pinch of salt and black pepper.
4. Blend until smooth, adding a little water if necessary to achieve the desired consistency.
5. Garnish with fresh parsley if desired and serve immediately, or store in the fridge for up to 3 days.

Nutritional Information (Per Serving):
Calories: 90 kcal | Total Fat: 5 g (Saturated Fat: 1 g) | Cholesterol: 0 mg | Fibre: 4 g | Protein: 2 g

Apple Cider Vinegar and Honey Dressing

Preparation Time: 5 minutes | **Servings:** 1small jar

Ingredients:
2 tablespoons apple cider vinegar
1 tablespoon honey
3 tablespoons olive oil
1 teaspoon Dijon mustard
Salt and black pepper to taste

Instructions:
1. In a small bowl, whisk together the apple cider vinegar, honey, olive oil, and Dijon mustard until well combined.
2. Season with salt and black pepper to taste.
3. Serve immediately or store in an airtight container in the fridge for up to 3 days. Shake or stir well before use.

Nutritional Information (Per Serving):
Calories: 100 kcal | Total Fat: 9 g (Saturated Fat: 1 g) | Cholesterol: 0 mg | Fibre: 0 g | Protein: 0 g

Lemon and Dill Sauce

Preparation Time: 5 minutes | **Servings:** 1 small bowl

Ingredients:
Juice of 1 lemon
2 tablespoons low-fat plain yoghurt
(or dairy-free alternative)
1 tablespoon olive oil
1 tablespoon fresh dill, chopped
1 garlic clove, minced
1 teaspoon Dijon mustard
Salt and black pepper to taste

Instructions:
1. In a small bowl, whisk together the lemon juice, yoghurt, olive oil, garlic, Dijon mustard, and chopped dill until well combined.
2. Season with salt and black pepper to taste.
3. Serve immediately or refrigerate for up to 2 days. Stir well before use.

Nutritional Information (Per Serving):
Calories: 60 kcal | Total Fat: 5 g (Saturated Fat: 1 g) | Cholesterol: 0 mg | Fibre: 0 g | Protein: 1 g

Garlic and Herb Yogurt Sauce

Preparation Time: 5 minutes   **Servings:** 1small bowl

Ingredients:
100 g low-fat plain yoghurt (or dairy-free alternative)
1 tablespoon olive oil
1 garlic clove, minced
1 tablespoon fresh parsley, chopped
1 tablespoon fresh chives, chopped
1 teaspoon lemon juice
½ teaspoon Dijon mustard
Salt and black pepper to taste

Instructions:
1. In a small bowl, mix together the yoghurt, olive oil, minced garlic, lemon juice, and Dijon mustard until smooth.
2. Stir in the chopped parsley and chives.
3. Season with salt and black pepper to taste.
4. Serve immediately or store in an airtight container in the fridge for up to 3 days. Stir well before use.

Nutritional Information (Per Serving):
Calories: 70 kcal | Total Fat: 4 g (Saturated Fat: 1 g) | Cholesterol: 0 mg | Fibre: 0 g | Protein: 4 g

Spiced Beetroot and Tahini Dip

Preparation Time: 10 minutes | **Cooking Time:** 30 minutes | **Servings:** 1small bowl

Ingredients:
2 medium beetroots, peeled and chopped
1 tablespoon olive oil
1 tablespoon tahini1 garlic clove, minced
1 tablespoon lemon juice
½ teaspoon ground cumin
½ teaspoon ground coriander
Salt and black pepper to taste
Fresh coriander leaves for garnish (optional)

Instructions:
1. Preheat the oven to 200°C (180°C fan) or gas mark 6.
2. Toss the chopped beetroot in olive oil and spread on a baking tray. Roast in the oven for 30 minutes or until tender.
3. Once roasted, transfer the beetroot to a food processor. Add the tahini, minced garlic, lemon juice, ground cumin, ground coriander, and a pinch of salt and black pepper.
4. Blend until smooth, adding a little water if necessary to achieve the desired consistency.
5. Garnish with fresh coriander leaves if desired, and serve immediately or store in the fridge for up to 3 days.

Nutritional Information (Per Serving):
Calories: 100 kcal | Total Fat: 6 g (Saturated Fat: 1 g) | Cholesterol: 0 mg | Fibre: 3 g | Protein: 2 g

Balsamic and Rosemary Reduction

Preparation Time: 5 minutes | **Cooking Time:** 10-12 minutes | **Servings:** 1small bowl

Ingredients:
100 ml balsamic vinegar
1 tablespoon honey or maple syrup
1 sprig fresh rosemary
1 garlic clove, minced
Salt and black pepper to taste

Instructions:
1. In a small saucepan, combine the balsamic vinegar, honey (or maple syrup), garlic, and the sprig of rosemary.
2. Bring the mixture to a simmer over medium heat and cook for 10-12 minutes, stirring occasionally, until it thickens and reduces by about half.
3. Remove the saucepan from the heat and discard the rosemary sprig.
4. Season with salt and black pepper to taste.
5. Let the sauce cool slightly before serving. It will continue to thicken as it cools.

Nutritional Information (Per Serving):
Calories: 50 kcal | Total Fat: 0 g (Saturated Fat: 0 g) | Cholesterol: 0 mg | Fibre: 0 g | Protein: 0 g

Bonus Chapter 2: Heart-Healthy Living Tips:

Eating Out and Staying Low Cholesterol

Eating out while sticking to a low cholesterol diet doesn't have to be tricky. With a few simple tips, you can enjoy meals out without worry.

First, check the menu ahead of time if possible. Many restaurants now list healthier options or allow you to see ingredients online. Look for dishes that are grilled, baked, or steamed rather than fried, and ask for sauces or dressings on the side so you can control how much you use.

Opt for lean proteins like chicken, turkey, or fish, and don't be shy about asking for swaps. Most places are happy to switch chips for a side salad or vegetables. Choose olive oil or vinegar dressings instead of creamy ones, and load up on colourful veg wherever you can.

Finally, don't forget portion control. Restaurants often serve larger portions than we need, so consider sharing a dish or taking some home for later.

By making small adjustments, you can still enjoy your favourite restaurants while keeping your cholesterol in check!

How to Manage Your Cholesterol During Holidays and Special Occasions

Holidays and special occasions often mean big meals and tempting treats, but you can still manage your cholesterol without missing out on the fun.

Start by being mindful of portions. It's easy to go overboard, but try to fill your plate with a balance of lean proteins, vegetables, and whole grains. Keep the richer, higher-fat options as smaller side portions, so you can enjoy a bit of everything.

When it comes to appetisers or nibbles, go for veggie sticks, hummus, or a handful of nuts instead of fried snacks or pastries. If you're contributing to a meal, why not bring a healthy dish? That way, you'll know there's a low-cholesterol option available.

It's also a good idea to watch your alcohol intake, as some drinks are high in calories and can lead to overeating. Opt for sparkling water, or limit yourself to one or two glasses of wine.

Lastly, don't stress! Special occasions are meant to be enjoyed, so if you do indulge, just get back on track the next day with healthy meals and plenty of exercise.

With a little planning, you can celebrate and still keep your cholesterol levels in check!

Supplements for Lowering Cholesterol

While a balanced diet and regular exercise are key to managing cholesterol levels, some people may also benefit from using supplements. However, it's important to remember that any supplements should only be taken after consulting your doctor or healthcare professional to ensure they are safe and suitable for you. Below are a few commonly suggested supplements that may help lower cholesterol:

1. **Plant Sterols and Stanols**: These naturally occurring substances can block the absorption of cholesterol in the intestines, helping to lower LDL (bad) cholesterol levels. They are often found in fortified foods or available as supplements.

2. **Omega-3 Fatty Acids**: Found in fish oil or flaxseed oil supplements, omega-3s can help reduce triglycerides, another type of fat in the blood that can raise the risk of heart disease.
3. **Soluble Fibre Supplements**: Psyllium husk, found in fibre supplements, can help reduce LDL cholesterol by binding to cholesterol in the digestive system and preventing its absorption.
4. **Garlic Supplements**: Garlic has long been suggested for its heart health benefits, and some studies indicate it may help lower cholesterol. However, the effect is generally mild and should be used with a doctor's advice.
5. **Red Yeast Rice**: This traditional Chinese supplement contains natural compounds similar to statins, which help lower cholesterol. However, it should only be used under the guidance of a healthcare professional due to possible side effects.
6. **Niacin (Vitamin B3)**: Niacin can raise HDL (good) cholesterol and lower LDL cholesterol and triglycerides. However, high doses can cause side effects, so it's important to only take it under medical guidance.

While supplements may support cholesterol management, they should be part of a broader lifestyle approach that includes healthy eating, exercise, and professional medical advice. Always check with your doctor before starting any new supplements, especially if you are on medication or have underlying health conditions.

Non-Cooking Tips for a Healthier Heart

Beyond food, there are many surprising ways to look after your heart. Here are some non-cooking tips that might not be on your radar:

1. Laugh More
It's true – laughter really is good for your heart! Studies show that a good laugh can lower stress hormones, reduce inflammation in your arteries, and increase good cholesterol (HDL). Whether it's watching a comedy or spending time with friends, don't underestimate the power of laughter.

2. Spend Time in Nature
Being outdoors and connecting with nature can lower blood pressure and stress levels, both of which contribute to a healthy heart. A walk in the park, a trip to the countryside, or even a few minutes in your garden can work wonders for your wellbeing.

3. Pet Therapy
If you're an animal lover, spending time with pets can benefit your heart health. Studies suggest that pet owners tend to have lower blood pressure and cholesterol levels. Even a few minutes of stroking a cat or playing with a dog can help reduce stress.

4. Cold Showers
Taking a cold shower might sound uncomfortable, but cold exposure can stimulate blood circulation, help reduce inflammation, and give your cardiovascular system a mini workout. Start with a few seconds of cold water at the end of your shower and gradually increase the time.

5. Get Creative
Engaging in creative activities like painting, knitting, or even journaling can have a calming effect on your mind and body. These activities promote relaxation, which can lower heart rate and blood pressure. Plus, the focus required helps to shift your mind away from stress.

6. Stand Up More
Sitting for long periods isn't great for your heart. Even if you exercise regularly, too much sitting can still pose a risk. Try standing up and moving around every 30 minutes – whether it's walking around the house, stretching, or even doing some light chores.

7. Singing
Singing, whether in the shower or along to the radio, can be great for your heart. It helps regulate your breathing, reduces stress, and can improve circulation. Plus, if you're singing with others, it builds social connections, which are also great for your heart.

Appendix: Measurement Conversions

This appendix provides helpful conversions for measurements commonly used in cooking, converting from British measurements to those commonly used internationally.

Weight
- 28 grams (g) = 1 ounce (oz)
- 454 grams = 16 ounces = 1 pound (lb)

Volume (Liquid)
- 5 millilitres (ml) = 1 teaspoon (tsp)
- 15 millilitres = 1 tablespoon (tbsp)
- 28 millilitres = 1 fluid ounce (fl oz)
- 240 millilitres = 1 cup
- 568 millilitres = 1 pint
- 1.14 litres = 1 quart
- 4.55 litres = 1 gallon

Volume (Dry Ingredients)
Dry measurements can vary depending on the ingredient, but for general guidance:
- 120 grams = 1 cup flour
- 200 grams = 1 cup sugar
- 90 grams = 1 cup oats
- 227 grams = 1 cup butter

Temperature
- To convert from Celsius (°C) to Fahrenheit (°F): multiply by 9/5, then add 32.
Example: 180°C × 9/5 = 324. Add 32 = 356°F.
- Common oven temperatures:
    - 120°C = 250°F
    - 150°C = 300°F
    - 180°C = 350°F
    - 200°C = 400°F
    - 230°C = 450°F

Length
- 2.54 centimetres (cm) = 1 inch (in)

Baking Tin Sizes
- 20 cm round tin = 8-inch round tin
- 23 cm square tin = 9-inch square tin

For additional guidance, consider using a kitchen scale or measuring cups for the most accurate results. Happy cooking!

Printed in Dunstable, United Kingdom